Jerome Doraisamy is a lawyer and writer from Sydney, NSW. He left legal practice in 2015 to publish his first book, *The Wellness Doctrines for Law Students and Young Lawyers*, which peaked at #2 on iTunes and has been sold, in both paperback and eBook form, on all six continents. He currently works as a journalist for *Lawyers Weekly*, and is an adjunct law lecturer at the University of Western Australia. In his spare time, Jerome is an avid reader, podcast listener, cake baker and F45 convert, and also plays indoor soccer and mixed netball every week. *The Wellness Doctrines for High School Students* is his second book.

Jerome Doraisamy is a lawyer and writer from Sydney, NSW. He left legal practice in 2015 to publish his first book, *The Wellness Doctrines for Law Students and Young Lawyers*, which peaked at #2 on iTunes and has been sold, in both paperback and eBook form, in all six continents. He currently works as a journalist for *Lawyers Weekly*, and is an adjunct law lecturer at the University of Western Australia. In his spare time, Jerome is an avid cricket [illegible] cake baker and [illegible], and also plays indoor soccer and mixed netball every week. *The Wellness Doctrines for High School Students* is his second book.

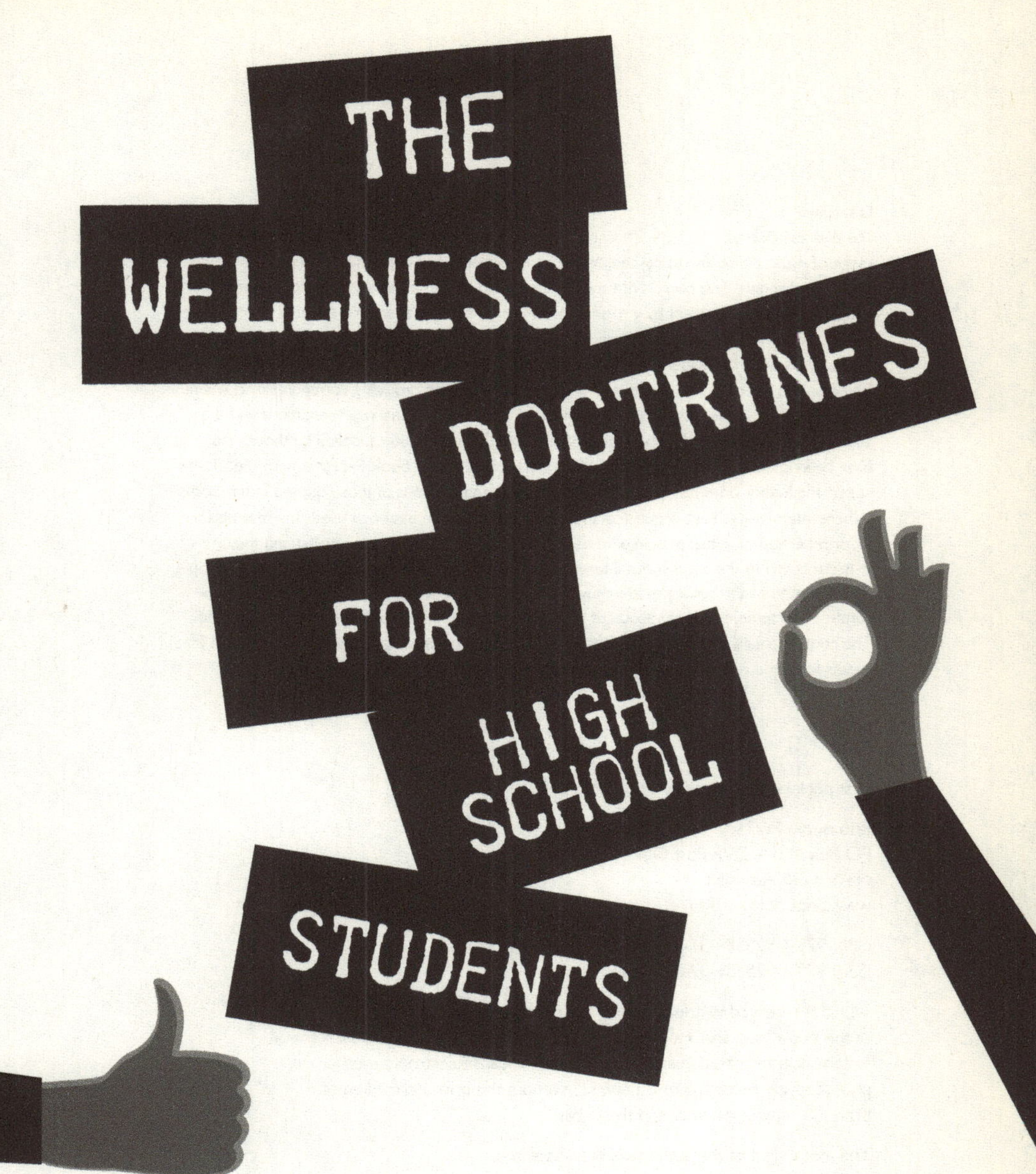

Jerome Doraisamy

Disclaimer

The Wellness Doctrines for High School Students is a practical self-help guide that addresses a range of issues pertaining to psychological distress, anxiety and depression in the secondary educational sphere. This book is not meant nor should it be used as a substitute for consultation with, diagnosis, or treatment by, a medical professional. It offers anecdotal experience and advice of those who have been through high school and/or work within high schools, as well as strategies and solutions for readers that have been discussed with mental health experts.

The opinions expressed by the author and those interviewed providing comments or opinions are theirs alone. These views are not intended to be truthful, factual representations and the author is not responsible for the accuracy of any of the information supplied by those who have been interviewed and/or whose comments appear in this book. Except where specifically stated, the author does not endorse the statements and opinions of those quoted in this book. Where interviewees have requested anonymity, a pseudonym has been used. Any resemblance to, or reflection of, actual people who bear those names is entirely coincidental and the opinions attributed to the anonymous interviewees should not be attributed to those actual people. References to health resources are provided for informational purposes only and do not constitute endorsement of such resources over other existing outlets unless otherwise specified. The contact details were correct at the time of printing, however readers should be aware that details for some resources might have changed following publication of this book.

First published in Xoum by Brio Books in 2018

Brio Books Pty Ltd
PO Box Q324, QVB Post Office,
NSW 1230, Australia
www.briobooks.com.au

ISBN 978-1-925589-31-3 (print)
ISBN 978-1-925589-32-0 (digital)

Cataloguing-in-publication data is available from the National Library of Australia

Cover design by Xou Creative, www.xoucreative.com.au
Printed and bound in Australia by McPherson's Printing Group

Papers used by Brio Books are natural, recyclable products made from wood grown in sustainable forests. The manufacturing processes conform to the environmental regulations of the country of origin.

Contents

Testimonials

"High school should be the best time in a teenager's life. But the reality is for some kids it's a nightmare. This book is full of proper advice about dealing with the big stuff, not sweating the small stuff … and nailing it by graduation day." **Karl Stefanovic (Co-host, TODAY show)**

"We know so much more about mental health than when I was a teenager. I wish people talked about mental self-care back then." **John Brogden (CEO, Lifeline)**

"We need to make mental health our number one priority. This book gives great insight into recognising, acknowledging and dealing with the pressures of being a high school student." **Bernard Foley (Australian Wallabies and NSW Waratahs player)**

"A must for all high school students and their parents. A great guide to navigate a time in our lives that we need some help with." **Gus Worland (host, "The Grill Team", Triple M)**

"Based on his own personal mental health journey, Jerome Doraisamy provides practical and easy ways for you to proactively look after your mental health while going through some of the most challenging times of your life." **Sam Refshauge (CEO, batyr)**

"*The Wellness Doctrines* is the kind of resource I wish that I had when I was growing up and juggling the stress of social pressure and academic demands." **Danny Clayton (TV and radio host)**

"The positive ripple effect of sharing lived experience is unquantifiable. It can create hope to those suffering in silence. Jerome's story of hope will no doubt help at least one person which is a success no matter which way you look at it." **Sam Webb (co-founder, Livin.org)**

"Having read Jerome Doraisamy's *The Wellness Doctrines for Law Students and Young Lawyers*, I know that this new book, for teenagers at school, will be an essential tool for guiding them through a time in their life when things can become overwhelming and challenging." **Alistair McEwin (Disability Discrimination Commissioner, Australian Human Rights Commission)**

"It's great to see passionate young people wanting to use their own experiences to help their peers. Through sharing real and relevant experiences Jerome has the ability to provide meaningful and practical advice for young people." **Dr Michelle Blanchard (General Manager, SANE Australia)**

"When it comes to managing your mental health there is no secret answer or shortcut. It is a combination of education, tools, coping strategies and strong support networks. *The Wellness Doctriness for High School Students* encapsulates these theories and is a valuable resource in improving mental health literacy and management." **Dan Hunt (retired NRL player; founder, Mental Health Movement)**

"A timely reminder of a number of the fundamental things that are easily forgotten in an increasingly noisy world. To be kind to yourself. To put down your phone. To engage with others and the world around you. To live life to the fullest." **Pat McCabe (retired Australian Wallabies and ACT Brumbies player)**

"A must-have in helping adequately support both parents and students in creating the environment where teens look after themselves … for the benefit of all." **Dan Collins (4 x Olympian, silver and bronze Olympic medallist)**

"Jerome's book is a must-read for all teachers and students. It offers sound advice on how to manage day-to-day stresses by giving first-hand experiences." **Bridie Duggan (Northern Territory Young Australian of the Year 2017)**

"Jerome draws on evidence and advice from many experts to provide practical tips that work. It is a valuable roadmap to help you to thrive, by focusing on the things you can control." **Graeme Cowan (Board Director, R U OK?; author, *Back From The Brink* series)**

"Jerome has established himself as one of the most renowned mental health advocates in Australia. His latest book adds to his growing legacy and outstanding body of work by once again raising awareness and creating conversation about one of the most important topics in the world today." **Danny Baker (bestselling author, *Depression is a Liar* and *I Will Not Kill Myself, Olivia*)**

"Jerome continues his courageous, vulnerable and transparent self-disclosure journey to provide a much needed, easily digestible, and practical resource for teenagers to help them become familiar with, and take charge of, their own mental health needs and wants." **Rebecca Michalak (principal, PsychSafe)**

"Jerome lights the way toward understanding and dealing with negative thoughts and the hard times that come with them. He equips us with the tools and wisdom to keep ourselves in the light. A must-read for the modern teenager." **Jim Finn (Art vs Science)**

"It is vitally important that we all play a part in ensuring children are properly educated about how to cope with mental ill health and how to overcome challenges they may face later in their lives. I am sure Jerome's book with help to achieve this." **Zoie Carroll (Founder, Zottie Dottie; 2017 Queensland Young Achiever of the Year for Leadership)**

"Jerome Doraisamy cuts through to the truth about teenage depression with sensitivity and honesty. His story is a reminder that mental illness touches all of us in some way, at some time. That's why this isn't just important for students feeling the pressure, but their teachers and families as well." **Angie Asimus (Seven News presenter)**

"An insightful, honest and inspiring resource – not just for students – but for everyone." **Anna Lisle (author, chef; former contestant, *My Kitchen Rules*)**

"Jerome perfectly weaves his own experience of mental illness into an honest handbook for students. It's a conversation that is much needed for future leaders of our world." **Sarah Whyte (Walkley Award-winning journalist)**

"In his open style, Jerome Doraisamy gives us a frank and practical guide to seeing ourselves more clearly, bearing the burden of our anxieties and insecurities, and finding the path back to wellness." **Matthew Pearson (Director and COO, Fleet Space Technologies)**

"This information is not only important for students in high school, but for them to take forward into careers in all industries – and I can vouch the performing arts needs it. If you don't have an experience with anxiety, someone you know will." **Madeleine Kazda (Miss Universe Australia finalist; professional dancer)**

"*The Wellness Doctrines* is a valuable resource in maintaining balance, taking the pressure off yourself and having fun – life is always meant to be enjoyed!" **Marshall Dunn (author, *Letters to Mitch*; host, "Straight From The Source's Mouth" podcast)**

"Jerome Doraisamy has once again got people talking with this refreshing manual for taking care of yourself in high school. A sincere, powerful and often funny guide to keeping your head screwed on during one of the most testing periods of your life." **Daniel Piotrowski (senior reporter, *Daily Mail Australia*)**

Author's note

"High school years are some of the hardest of your life. Know that I feel your pain, and that it does get easier," Mitch Wallis said.

One in five adolescents will have experienced depression by the time they turn 18[1]. Over 75% of mental health problems occur before the age of 25[2]. And – perhaps most troubling – young people are less likely than any other age group to seek professional help[3].

Too many students who experience psychological distress, anxiety, depression and other mental illnesses suffer in silence. Having experienced anxiety and depression personally, I would not wish mental health issues upon anyone, least of all high school students.

High schools across the country are getting better at looking after their charges, introducing in-class positive psychology programs, for example. But health and wellbeing isn't taught, as a life lesson, in the same way that we learn English, maths or geography.

"If we can be taught about cellular structures, poetic devices and the marital customs of the ancient Romans, is it really too much to ask to also be taught about maintaining good mental health?"

This hypothetical question was posed to me by Sam C., who graduated from high school in Perth in 2015. It's a fair question. Why don't we learn about health and wellbeing as part of subjects or classes that teach us more about life and how to live it?

Popular American blogger Mark Manson simply had this to say on the subject: "Let's be honest: our education system is f*cked"[4].

While I don't agree with Mark's blunt take on things, he does have a point. He went on to say that in his opinion high school needs to do better when it comes to preparing students for life. Kids should be taught more about personal finances and tax, how to manage relationships (romantic and professional), logic and reasoning, self-awareness and scepticism[5]. All of these topics are – believe it or not – linked to our overall health and wellbeing.

One day, those who run our schools may offer extra health and wellbeing lessons for secondary students, building on the great work they already do. But until then, you need to find ways to help yourself and – where possible – those around you.

That's where this book comes in.

The Wellness Doctrines for High School Students is a self-help guide, or "pocket survival guide", for teenagers to help them proactively and preemptively manage their health and wellbeing. The issues are as expansive as they are individual to each person's experience.

Practical solutions and strategies are offered to arm you with the tools you need to be as healthy and happy as you can. Throughout the book, you'll also find "Wellbeing Wisdom" sections which summarise the preceding chapter with dot point takeaways for ease of reference.

The Wellness Doctrines for High School Students is dedicated to every student coming through the ranks who feels ill-equipped, underappreciated or alone in dealing with the struggles they face. I promise you: you are none of those things. I hope this book serves as a helpful guide in navigating your way to optimal health and happiness and, ultimately, success in school and beyond.

Recorded interviews were conducted with dozens of individuals from across the community, including high school principals, teachers, careers counsellors, psychologists, students and their parents, and mental health experts. These interviewees shared their own experiences, what they witnessed in their friends, classmates, subordinates, patients or children, and what they think can be done to improve the experience of high school students.

Not all interviewees had experienced health issues themselves; rather, they were encouraged to provide broader perspectives into how such issues can and do affect teenagers, and subsequently their progression through secondary education.

Some interviewees are named, whereas others opted for anonymity (and thus have been given pseudonyms).

Regardless of whether or not an interviewee has been named, I am grateful to all of them; they showed great courage in speaking with me.

INTERVIEWEES FEATURED IN THIS BOOK INCLUDE:

- Alicia (student, using a pseudonym)
- Amba Brown (positive psychology author)
- Camellia (high school tutor)
- Chelsea (student)
- Chris (pastoral care educator)
- Debbie (parent)
- Eileen Condell (psychotherapist and counsellor for young people)
- Flynne (student)
- Holly G. (high school tutor)
- Holly M. (student)
- Dr Jenny Brockis (brain health and mind performance specialist)
- Katie Bennett (careers coach)
- Professor Lina Ricciardelli (psychologist, eating disorders expert)
- Lisa Farrow (school psychologist)
- Louka Parry (former school principal and Director of Programs, Education Changemakers)
- Luke Furness (CEO, Out for Australia)
- Maria (parent)
- Milly (student)

- Mitch Wallis (founder, Heart On My Sleeve)
- Natalie (parent)
- Dr Nicola Lipscombe (mindfulness expert)
- Peter (parent)
- Dr Pree Benton (health psychologist specialising in eating disorders)
- Rachael (parent)
- Sam C. (student)
- Sam D. (parent and educator)
- Sophia (student)
- Sophie (educator)
- Steve (parent and educational psychologist)
- Dr Tim Sharp ("Dr Happy", TWD psychology expert)
- Tony (parent)

Ten per cent of the profits from sales of this book will be donated to batyr, an organisation that aims to engage, educate and empower young people to have positive conversations about mental health. Chief among batyr's activities are lectures and workshops for high schools across Australia, which bridge the gap between individual suffering and resource seeking. batyr gives a voice to the elephant in the room.

Just as this book aims to do.

Expert's note: Dr Tim Sharp (aka Dr Happy)

Dr Happy is an internationally-renowned leader in the field of positive psychology. He boasts three degrees in psychology (including a PhD) and is the founder & CHO (Chief Happiness Officer) of The Happiness Institute, Australia's first organisation devoted solely to enhancing happiness in individuals, families and organisations.

If you've not experienced mental ill health directly, then you'll almost certainly experience it indirectly. That is, at some point in our lives, almost all of us will either experience moderate to severe stress, depression or anxiety; or if not, we'll know someone who has (a friend, family member, colleague or classmate). For the majority of people who suffer these forms of distress, the struggles start in high school (or soon after); which is why this book is so important.

High school is a time and place where we learn about many things. Hopefully with *The Wellness Doctrines for High School Students*, more teenagers will learn more about themselves and their moods. Because the good news is that even though many will suffer, there's much we can do to take control of our lives, to feel better, and/or to help others feel better. In fact, addressing our wellness proactively and positively is very possibly the most important thing we can do in life. It's my hope that this book will provide you with some suggestions to achieve this and to enjoy the benefits.

Jerome's journey

Imagine being at a stand-up comedy show.

You're seeing one of the most famous comedians in the world deliver a set at which everyone else in the audience is cracking up, some with tears of laughter streaming down their face. You're surrounded by people who are having a great time, whereas you feel … nothing at all.

You were really looking forward to going to the show, and wish you could enjoy yourself just as everyone else is, but your heart and mind are numb. You just can't get into the swing of it. And you suddenly feel like you want to go home so that you can stop pretending to feel something other than emptiness.

Now, picture yourself trapped in a tank of deep, dark water.

You've been treading water for a long time, keeping your head above the surface, and you're exhausted. You're not sure how much longer you can keep it up, hoping that someone will come and rescue you from the depths. But no one does.

No one is coming to save you because nobody knows you're trapped in the tank. And despite all the treading of water you're doing, deep down you feel like you're not going to survive, and you lose all hope.

Finally, think about what it would be like to be imprisoned at Azkaban, the wizard prison in J.K. Rowling's *Harry Potter* novels. You're surrounded by Dementors, whose purpose is to suck out the happy memories from your life and leave you only with the bad ones. Unfortunately, you're not Sirius Black and can't morph into a black dog and swim to safety. You can't escape these soul-sucking creatures, and everything good and joyful in your life is slipping away before your very eyes.

(Of all the *Harry Potter* fantasies you may have had, I'm certain this is not one of them!)

However, for many people, this is precisely what depression feels like.

It's what it felt like for me.

Feeling numb and detached from the rest of the world. Feeling like you're struggling to survive. Feeling like there will never be anything good in your life again. When you suffer from depression, in its many forms, you'll experience these feelings and countless others.

I suffered from a major breakdown at New Year's in 2011 while at a music festival with my school friends. This kick-started an 18-month period of severe clinical depression and anxiety. In that moment of breakdown at the festival, I experienced all three of the above scenarios: I felt void of any joy or happiness, like that being experienced by my mates while listening to the music; and I felt like I was desperately trying to enjoy myself and unwind, but just couldn't escape the dark hole I was in. If I couldn't have fun at a music festival with my best mates, then how could I ever be happy anywhere else?

While my breakdown occurred during – and largely as a result of – issues at law school, a lot of the problems I suffered started back in high school.

I graduated from St Aloysius' College, a private Catholic boys' school, in 2005. Aloys is founded on and lives by the Jesuit tradition, espousing the need to be "a man for others" and serve the community – values I try to retain to this day. I have a close-knit group of about 20 mates, whom I see at least every couple of weeks, if not weekly. I am lucky to have such a friendship circle; the fact that I am writing this 12 years after we graduated speaks volumes about those connections.

Being part of such a community made my high school experience memorable. But school was not without its challenges. I was driven to succeed and placed a lot of importance on both my academic marks and my sporting achievements. If I didn't achieve a certain grade on an essay or exam, I thought it was a personal failure. I constantly compared myself to those around me. Becoming a school prefect was not something I was proud of; it was simply a marker through which I could claim some sense of self-worth. I relentlessly pushed myself to be number one … anything less just wasn't good enough.

Having such an approach didn't result in any kind of psychological or emotional breakdown (at the time). Looking back, I'm amazed I didn't crash and burn. And it's perhaps because I didn't suffer any lasting consequences, and instead managed to achieve most everything I wanted at school, that

I took those same attitudes with me to law school, where the issues compounded.

At university, I continued to push myself to the point of physical abuse. In the two years leading up to my breakdown in 2011, I was studying full-time, working two or three days a week as a paralegal at a property law firm, volunteering 30–35 hours a week as vice president of the law students' society, and surviving on four or five hours of sleep a night. Ultimately, it wasn't sustainable.

Even having taken a gap year – I spent seven months on a remote island in Vanuatu, living in a bamboo hut overlooking the water and teaching English and maths in a local high school – my underlying stresses and anxieties remained, waiting to surface.

I couldn't recognise what I was going through. At high school, I was unaware of anxiety and depression, and the signs and symptoms. Because I wasn't able to understand or appreciate the dangers, my issues worsened, until I ultimately broke down with one semester of university to go. Getting through those final subjects was torture. My capacity to take up a graduate job was shot.

Why am I telling you all of this?

I believe it is important to share my experiences with you for a number of reasons.

Firstly, it is necessary to feature and provide insight into the struggles of those suffering from depression. By doing so, I hope that some, if not all of you, will be able to feel connected to what I know to be a common story.

Secondly, I want to instil in you a sense of confidence and comfort in talking about these issues. By candidly discussing my own story (even if it happened after I'd already finished school), I hope to inspire you. Of course, this does not mean that every high school student who has depression should go out and broadcast their experiences by writing a book! Rather, my goal is to make those living with these conditions feel safe enough to speak up and seek help, without fear of negative consequences.

Finally, I am writing this so that we can all draw strength from the fact that things *can* get better. No matter how bad you feel, no matter how awful things may appear, don't ever forget that things *can* get better. For me, it did. And with the right care, support and action, it will for you too. I truly hope that you can take something useful from this book, whether it is my story or my experiences, or the experiences of others.

At the very least, please give consideration to what is written here. After all, it could save your life, just as it did mine.

Why should I even care about my mental health?

Some of you may have picked up this book because your parents bought it for you, or your school made you read it, and now you're wondering, "Why do I need to know about mental health problems? I'm perfectly healthy and happy, and I don't need this."

Maybe that's true. Maybe you won't ever suffer anxiety or depression.

But … one in five young people *will* have experienced depression by the time they reach 18 years of age[6]. And over 75% of mental health problems occur before the age of 25[7].

Mental health issues such as anxiety and depression are

among the biggest hurdles to be faced by young people going through high school. For our nation's Indigenous population, these issues are even more pronounced. And for the LGBTQI community, their mental health – regardless of age – remains among the poorest in Australia[8].

> Young people are less likely than any other age group to seek professional help[9].

If you're an Australian student reading this, you will likely have heard of the phrase, "SLIP, SLOP, SLAP".

It's the advice we are given, from an early age, to protect ourselves from skin cancers and melanoma when we go outside. Because of Australia's geographical climate and exposure to ultra-violet rays, we are more susceptible to the sun than people in other countries, and we therefore accept the sound medical advice.

As a high school student, you need to apply the same logic.

Right now, you're dealing with a lot: changes to your body; changes to your relationships with family and friends; you've got questions about your future, you want to fit in … and probably stuff I wouldn't even know about.

Because of everything you have going on, it's necessary to put in place certain safeguards to ensure you are feeling on top of life and as balanced as possible.

Another way of looking at it is to consider the example of a professional sportsperson. Let's think about the Australian sportswoman, Ellyse Perry. By virtue of her job, Ellyse has to stretch intensely before stepping onto the field to avoid getting injured if she over-exerts herself.

Stretching doesn't guarantee Ellyse won't get injured, but it makes her more flexible and therefore less likely to get hurt. Because she plays sport every day – and gets paid well to do so – it's important for her to make sure she's as healthy and fit as possible so that she can do her job properly.

The same logic applies to you. Because you're in an environment, and at a stage of life, where stress and anxiety are commonplace, you need to take *preventative* measures to look after yourself.

Of course, you may never get to a point where you need to seek help for mental health issues – in fact, I really hope you never have to!

But the reality is that many high school students will suffer from psychological distress, anxiety, depression or any number of mental health issues. In short: no one has 100%, perfect mental health; we all feel stressed from time to time.

In high school, as we undergo massive personal, emotional, social and physical changes, while approaching final exams before heading out into the wider world, our susceptibility to stress is increased. And stress – while sometimes only fleeting – can manifest into much larger problems if we don't look after ourselves.

YOU NEED TO BE ABLE TO:

- **Recognise the prevalence and dangers of mental health issues; and**

- **Take steps to manage and combat any issues that give rise to such health issues, so that you can be as healthy and happy as possible.**

So how do you do this?

Be *proactive*, rather than *reactive*!

You can proactively do things to make yourself healthier and happier, rather than simply reacting to a situation, such as falling ill. Putting in place preventative measures is the best possible way you can avoid issues such as burnout, prolonged distress, anxiety and depression.

To be proactive about health and happiness, you need a way to monitor your daily and weekly activities and ensure each aspect of your life is serving the right purpose. For me, this means thinking of my life as a stable table-top.

The table-top is your health and wellbeing, and the legs of the table are what you use to prop yourself up. The more legs you have, the more stable your table-top is going to be. In my life, I have a leg for family, a leg for friends, a leg for work, sports, fitness, reading books, listening to music, cooking and baking, and so on. And the more time and energy I put into each one of those legs, the more likely it is that those legs are going to remain in place, and my health and wellbeing will be secure.

On the other hand, if I only have time for the leg of work, and if I'm not able to give any time or energy to the other legs, then it's highly likely that my table-top is going to fall over.

As a high school student, make time for more than just the leg of homework and study. Why? Here are just a few reasons:

- **To keep your table-top stable and secure**. As the above analogy demonstrates, creating balance will help you stay on track and in control. Having tunnel vision about what needs to be done will put you at greater risk of crashing and burning.

- **To ensure productivity and success at school**. It seems strange to think that doing even more, on top of your already-busy schedule, will make things easier. But having things to look forward to once you finish your homework and study for the night, such as a good book, a run around the block or a yoga session, allows you to disconnect from the stress of the day. It helps you unwind and relax, so that you can recharge your batteries when you go to sleep, and therefore wake up refreshed. If you're not able to switch off at the end of the day, you're not going to be at your best when you return to school.

- **To make life more enjoyable**. Doing things that bring pleasure and purpose makes our daily and weekly experience more fun. And given how hard high school can be, you could definitely do with more fun. So why not make it non-negotiable?

"You don't want to wait until it's a bigger problem before you tell someone or do something about it, because that's only going to make it harder for you to resolve," said Chelsea, who graduated from high school in Western Australia in 2015.

You may never suffer from any mental health issues. I really hope that you don't. But a lot of teenagers do. Taking the time to look after ourselves before such issues arise is the best way to ensure that we are as healthy and happy as we can be, and – as a result – as productive and successful at school as possible. It's ultimately in your self-interest to *proactively* look after your health and wellbeing ... so go out and do it!

"Mentally healthy students are well-performing students," said Holly G., a high school tutor in Perth.

ISSUES

There are heaps of issues – both big and small – that will stress you out, make you anxious, cause you grief and affect your health and wellbeing.

It's important that you know what these issues are, so that you can deal with them if they ever arise.

Listed in the next section of this book is a range of issues you might come across. I've included comments and advice from your peers, their parents, some teachers and other experts, so that you can have a better idea of what others have been through, and what they suggest you should do.

This section is by no means exhaustive … but learning about these particular issues will make you well placed to handle any and all other issues in your path.

Signs and symptoms

If you break your leg, it's pretty easy to recognise that there's a problem. With mental health, it's not always as easy to understand and appreciate what is going on, because having anxiety, depression or feeling suicidal isn't something that you can necessarily see on the surface.

As a result, it's critical to know the signs and symptoms of such mental health issues.

Sometimes, displaying these traits will just be part of growing up, or part of the high school cycle. But if you're showing these signs and symptoms[10] [11] [12] on a regular basis, or over a long period of time, then you need to be speaking to someone.

- **Feelings:** Overwhelmed, guilty, irritable, frustrated, panicked, lacking in confidence, unhappy, indecisive, disappointed, miserable, sad, low, flat, impatient, loss of temper, lacking motivation or purpose, suicidal.

- **Thoughts:** "I don't want to get out of bed in the morning", "I can't be bothered", "Everything is too hard", "I'm a failure", "It's my fault", "I can't do anything right", "Nothing good ever happens to me", "Life's not worth living", "People would be better off without me".

- **Behaviour:** Avoiding situations which make you anxious or uncomfortable, or activities that would usually be fun or make you happy, not going out anymore, withdrawing from family and friends, neglecting personal responsibilities, relying on alcohol or sedatives, not being productive with schoolwork, trouble doing well in school.

- **Physical signs:** Panic attacks, hot or cold flushes, racing heartbeat, tightening of the chest, rapid breathing, restlessness, feeling tense, wound up or edgy, unable to sleep, skin breakouts, constantly tired, sick or run down, having headaches or muscle pains, churning gut or stomach aches, loss or change of appetite, significant weight loss or gain, self-harm or harms others.

- **Psychological signs:** Excessive fear, worry, obsessive thinking, thinking everything is worse than it actually is, inability to concentrate, can't see the positives in life.

Signs and symptoms for eating disorders and related issues are listed in the Having a healthy body and diet chapter. You can also check out some of my own personal signs and symptoms, and how I deal with them, in the #triggered chapter. If you are ever in need of support, you can find – towards the end of this book – a list of websites, apps, programs and organisations in the Resources chapter.

Understanding anxiety and depression

"I would always see girls, in my year and above, in the playground with teachers, having a breakdown. I think everyone kind of associated it with the idea that, 'It's Year 12 … it's going to happen.'"

Anxiety can be so consuming that you feel like you just can't function.

It gets in the way of enjoying life. It can be a feeling of imminent disaster (such as being in an exam and not knowing anything), an overwhelming sense of worry (perhaps you fear being humiliated in front of your classmates), or just general concerns of embarrassment[13].

With depression, you have to be careful with who you make friends with because some people make you feel more insecure than you already are. They'll make you think that no one could ever like you. And that's really easy to believe when you look in the mirror and don't even like yourself[14].

Debbie, a mother of three from Brisbane, Queensland, told me about how anxiety overtook one of her daughters when she entered Year 11.

"My second daughter was extremely frightened by her anxiety, as she had never experienced anything like it before," she said. "She thought there was something physically wrong with her, and wanted to be taken to hospital to be checked out. She found it all extremely overwhelming, which only brought home to me how much my elder daughter must have felt as she suffered (and continues to suffer) through her own anxiety."

Sometimes, it is only when anxiety manifests in outbursts or physical symptoms that we are able to recognise what might be happening.

Part of the problem here is that all of us feel anxious at different times. No one has perfect mental health; we all feel stressed on occasion. It's natural and, to an extent, important that we experience such emotions, as it can positively kick-start our motivation to work hard and do well.

Thirty-two per cent of Aboriginal and Torres Strait Islander youths are at risk of serious mental illness, compared to 22% of the non-ATSI population[15].

But the danger of such thoughts and feelings depends on how strong they are. Making the distinction between what might be a healthy bout of worry versus stress and anxiety that is detrimental to our wellbeing is not easy.

Anxiety, to the point of breakdown, should never be accepted as normal. But Milly, who attended high school in Sydney, said witnessing such breakdowns was not unusual, nor was it supposedly a cause for alarm.

"You would always see girls, in my year and above, in the playground with teachers, having a breakdown. I think everyone kind of associated it with the idea that, 'It's Year 12 … it's going to happen,'" she said.

For Holly M., who graduated in New South Wales in 2014, the low to moderate levels of distress she experienced in the early years of high school grew into "full-blown anxiety" during Years 11 and 12.

"It got pretty bad … the thought of deadlines completely paralysed me and often led to me pulling all-nighters," she said. "I remember sitting in my music class, frozen in front of the computer while everyone else was working away on their compositions. I, on the other hand, had done nearly nothing and couldn't bear the thought of my teacher and peers seeing that. Ideas came to me quickly but distress about deadlines forbade me from putting them to use until it was nearly too late."

Over 36% of trans and over 24% of gay, lesbian and bisexual Australians screen positive for a major depressive

> episode, compared to just under 7% of the general population. Further, homosexual and bisexual Australians are more than twice as likely as their heterosexual peers to experience anxiety disorders (31% versus 14%)[16].

Seventy-five per cent of young people aged 15–19 who have a probable serious mental illness say that they are extremely concerned about coping with stress, and almost 60% of them are very concerned about depression[17]. And, among teenagers of the same age group who have no probable mental illnesses, over one-third are extremely concerned about their stress levels, and 14% are worried about depression[18].

In short, even among those who are healthy and happy, stress and depression is a big concern. The stats bear repeating: a fifth of all teenagers will have experienced depression by the time they reach 18 years of age[19]. Three quarters of mental health problems occur before the age of 25[20]. And the most troubling fact is that young people are *less* likely than any other age group to seek professional help[21].

According to Lisa Farrow, a school psychologist in Queensland, a mental health problem can overwhelm every aspect of your life.

"It can impact significantly upon lifestyle factors such as sleep, exercise and diet. This further impacts on their ability to regulate their emotions," she said.

Flynne from Melbourne suffered from depression throughout high school.

"I just didn't feel like myself anymore. When people hear 'depression', they think of someone who is sad all the time. I'm not sad all the time, I'm actually rarely sad. Depression is more empty than sad. When I'm not going through depression though, I'm happy-go-lucky, I love being around friends, I just want to have a good time. Depression makes me flaky. It makes me late. It makes me not do work. It makes me procrastinate. It makes me stay in. It makes me feel alone and isolate myself. It makes me think everyone hates me, because I mean, how can anyone like me if I don't like me?"[22]

Sophia, who went to school in Sydney, experienced a range of issues, including an eating disorder.

"I was diagnosed with anorexia at the end of Year 8, and had it on and off for about six years as a result; but I've also had severe depression–anxiety issues," she said. "My anxiety really came back in the latter part of Year 11 and the start of Year 12 as I started to feel the pressure to succeed and to do well in high school."

For all of these people, the high school environment was a major catalyst in shaping their mental health experiences.

Milly summed it up well. "I think the pressure just got to me. I set myself unrealistic goals of what I wanted to achieve and it overwhelmed me. I got to a point where I felt like there was a monster in my face trying to pull out this demon. It is the most awful feeling and you feel so alone and isolated. You're sad and you might laugh and you think, 'I can't laugh. I'm depressed. Why am I doing that?'"

Too often, high school students don't realise that anxiety and depression are just ailments that you experience … they don't reflect who you are as a person. There are ways through these conditions, and even if it takes a long time, it does *not* define you as a person, let alone the rest of your life.

TWD WELLBEING WISDOM

Mental health issues are among the fastest-growing illnesses in Australia. But, by taking certain steps to look after ourselves and those around us, we can put ourselves in the best possible position to stay healthy. If you are suffering from anxiety and depression – or if you want to avoid it – make sure you are doing the following:

- **Openly communicate about your life with people you trust**. A problem shared is a problem halved! Talk to your family and friends so that they can help you and so you can better understand what's going on.

- **Stay fit and active**. Exercise is key. Find physical activities that you like and that are convenient. Doing regular exercise will make you more energised for homework and study.

- **Know the signs and symptoms.** Learn about the trigger points for anxiety and depression, and be aware of your own personal indications of such mental health issues. Understanding these will give you warning about how you're going, and when you might need help.

- **Ensure proper downtime**. Always make time to rest up and relax. High school is a busy time, but it's a marathon, not a sprint. Be kind to yourself and have fun.

- **Get enough sleep.** Make sleep a priority so that you can stay as healthy as possible.

- **Take time to reflect and be mindful**. Take a step back and reflect on who you are, where you're at and where you're going. Mindful activities, in their many forms, can be useful for this.

- **Don't shut yourself off to different options**. If and when you experience mental health issues, be open to getting help – from wherever it comes.

- **Be aware of different issues that affect wellbeing**. Know what can make you sick, and what doesn't work when it comes to looking after yourself. Do some reading online, or ask around.

- **Know where you can seek help**. Educate yourself about the various resources available online, by telephone, and in person. These have helped countless people over the years, and could help you too.

AND ... FOR LGBTQI AND ATSI STUDENTS

While the wellness of LGBTQI and ATSI students may be more at risk than their cisgender heterosexual and/or non-Indigenous counterparts, there are ways that you can look after yourself if you feel that your health and wellbeing – and potentially your performance as well – is suffering as a result of your sexuality or cultural background.

Here are some ideas for you to seek support, both individually and in conjunction with others:

- **Remember, things will get better**. Just as life improves for any other student who struggles at high school, things will also get better for you. There is so much to look forward to once you walk out of those school gates for the last time.

- **You're not alone. Support exists – go find it**. There are more resources available to assist young LGBTQI or ATSI students than ever before ... take the time to research who and where they are, so that you can access help if and when you ever need it. Some of these are listed in the Resources chapter of this book.

- **Identify supportive people and confide in them**. In all likelihood, your friends will have your back if you allow them in. What matters is who you are as a friend to them ... the friends who matter won't change their minds about you, so don't be afraid to have that chat.

- **There is nothing wrong with your sexual orientation or cultural background**. The majority of your classmates will be heterosexual and non-Indigenous, but that doesn't mean that you are somehow abnormal. You are as worthy and valued as anyone else.

- **Be confident in your own skin, or with the colour of your skin**. It's much easier for bullies to target someone who doesn't own who they are. Don't self-stigmatise … be yourself and project confidence, even if you don't feel it.

- **But … always prioritise your own safety**. Nothing is more important than your personal wellbeing. Do only what makes you comfortable, to the extent that it caters to your physical, social and emotional wellness.

NB: all of these solutions and strategies are discussed in greater detail later in the book … head over to the table of contents to see exactly where you can learn more.

What you need to know about suicide and self-harm

"I was constantly contemplating the purpose of my being alive and was frequently Google-ing [sic] ways to kill myself. I got through it, though."

One in ten young Australians aged between 12–17 will self-harm, one in 13 will seriously consider a suicide attempt, and one in 40 young people will attempt suicide[23].

I remember a crushing sense of hopelessness. I remember feeling that the world was closing in around me, with down being the only direction. I remember plastering a smile on my face so that I wouldn't have to trouble others with my pain. I remember having my throat close up so that a scream became no more than a cough. I remember scheduling time into my day where I could break down and cry in private without interruption. I remember fearing that my family would never understand what I was going through, and therefore never understand me. I remember worrying that I was too great a burden for my friends to deal with, and that this burden would drive them away. I remember being in crowds of people yet still feeling totally alone. I remember feeling a complete and utter sense of detachment from the reality in which everyone else seemed to thrive. I remember thinking on numerous occasions that I had hit rock bottom only to discover, again and again, that there were no limits to just how far I could spiral.

> Intentional self-harm is the leading cause of death for Australians aged between 15–24, with over one young person committing suicide every day in Australia in 2015[24].

Too often, between late 2011 and mid-2013, I entertained the thoughts above. However, looking back, I am eternally grateful that even on my worst days, and in my darkest of moments, the thought of committing suicide never entered my mind.

I can therefore only imagine the unbearable, tortuous process of contemplating or even attempting suicide, or committing self-harm.

Young same-sex attracted Australian teenagers have up to six times higher rates of suicide attempts than their heterosexual peers[25].

Over 40% of Indigenous teens are worried about suicide and personal safety, compared to just over 30% of non-Indigenous persons[26].

"Unfortunately, our daughter started to self-harm, which was a really secretive thing for her and it took us a while to realise what was going on. It was about self-punishment," said Tony from Adelaide.

Sometimes, even that act of self-inflicted punishment can become something that you feel the need to do, in order to manage the issues you are facing.

In 2016, suicide rates for young Australians were at their highest levels in 10 years. Female suicide rates have doubled, and Aboriginal and Torres

Strait Islander youths in regional and remote areas are most at risk[27].

"The self-harm was really hard for me to get over, because it becomes quite addictive," Flynne said.

"It got to the point where I was so overwhelmed by school that I was constantly contemplating the purpose of my being alive and frequently Google-ing [sic] ways to kill myself. I got through it, though," said Holly M.

When one suicide occurs, others are twice as likely to follow at a youth level than they are with adults. One such "suicide cluster" identified by the report was in a remote central Queensland town, in which 21 young people committed suicide between 2010 and 2012[28].

If you are feeling suicidal or at the risk of self-harm, please talk to someone immediately. Don't suffer in silence. You are not alone and if you reach out, friends, family and others will be there for you. I promise that things *will* get better. But don't just take it from me … here is an excerpt from *Letters to Mitch*, a book written by a friend of mine, Marshall Dunn, whose elder brother Mitchell committed suicide:

"There is a way out of your pain. You are more than capable of doing it. Even in the the darkest of hours, there are healing discoveries that can take you to a different place. In my heart of hearts, I know there is an opportunity for you to feel good again. I know your heart is broken. You may be hurting so badly [that] you can't see a way out, but I promise you that there is one, and things will get better. In time, and with the willingness to get real with yourself and be present, you can heal your life."[29]

Even the idea of suicide – having thoughts about such an action or being concerned about it – is a dangerous place for a young person (or any person, for that matter). Of young Australians aged 15–19 who screened as having a probable mental illness, approximately one-third (32.3%) have great concerns about suicide.

TWD WELLBEING WISDOM

If you are having thoughts about suicide or self-harm, please do the following:

- **Talk to someone immediately.** Assistance is there if you ask for it. Not only are your parents, family members and friends available, but you can talk to your teachers, school counsellor, principal and GP, as well as numerous resources by phone or online.

- **OR ... go straight to hospital.** Being in the care of medical professionals at the emergency department can offer not only physical safety, but also a layer of emotional security for you.

- **Promise yourself you'll at least get through the night.** Pledge to not do anything to harm yourself today, and that you'll wait for tomorrow to come. Then make the same promise to get through to the following day.

- **Do something to distract yourself until help is at hand.** It's amazing how distracting a good song, or book, or an old movie can be when we're feeling depressed. Try writing down how you feel, setting yourself some tasks or making a "to do" list for tomorrow. Do something – *anything* – to take your mind off what you're currently feeling.

Also remember the following:

- **Suicide is *never* the answer.** Wanting to self-harm is a clear sign that, even if you believe you're thinking logically, something isn't right. Hurting yourself is *never* a solution to your problems.

- **You have family and friends who love you.** Just knowing you want to self-harm would be devastating to the people in your life. If you were to try anything, it would destroy them.

- **You are not alone.** Because those friends and family members care so much about you, they will always be there for you and have your back. You don't have to go through this by yourself.

- **Help is available.** There are resources for you at any hour of the day and on every medium – telephone, internet, in person, and so on. A few taps on your phone is all it takes.

- **The thoughts can and will pass.** You will likely never feel as bad as you do right now … which means that things can only get better. If you can survive this, you can survive anything.

- **You will be happy again.** It may seem like you're stuck in a hole with no ladder to get out. But there is *always* a way out. Happiness may seem like a long way away; it may take some time to find again. But you will find it and it will make your life richer than ever before.

Smashing the stigma about mental health

"You may feel like a broken individual in a million pieces. But you are still worthy of love – not just from other people, but also from yourself," Mitch Wallis said.

In a classroom of 30 students, around seven will be suffering from some form of mental illness. Of those seven, only two will feel comfortable speaking up about their struggles and seeking help. That means five kids in every class are suffering in silence[30].

In ancient Greece, slaves were marked in order to identify their position in the social structure and to indicate that they were of less value. These marks were referred to as *stizein*, from which we get the word *stigma* – a socially constructed term referring to a distinguishing mark of social disgrace, attached to others in order to identify and to devalue them[31].

Although the Greeks did not seem to have stigmatised the mentally ill, they nevertheless thought that being mentally ill carried a connotation of shame and weakness of character.

Things haven't changed much over the course of history.

Soldiers who suffer from post-traumatic stress disorder often do not receive the treatment they need. Popular culture and Hollywood still depict mentally ill persons as being "crazy" or in need of an asylum. Even the term "mental" has a negative connotation about it.

When I was at high school in the early 2000s, I was unaware of mental health issues. It wasn't something that was spoken about. Our idea of a mental breakdown, and what it might look like, would have come from movies or TV shows.

Growing up in that kind of environment has had long-term impacts upon how I talk with my schoolmates about these issues. They're all supportive, and want to see me well. But a lot of them don't really know how to talk about it.

It creates a different kind of stigma; one that means I may feel like I can't talk to my mates for fear of them not understanding, or not being able to offer anything constructive in response.

Things are improving … but there is still a long way to go.

Even in this day and age, 86% of working professionals would rather suffer in silence than tell their boss that they are struggling, for fear of being fired or passed over for promotion[32].

Fear of negative consequences not only reinforces a sense of isolation, but it stops you from seeking help from people who, ironically, would do anything to help you.

That fear of what other people may think can often lead to a sense of shame about what you're experiencing.

"I think kids are not seeking help because there's such a stigma around depression. Sometimes it can feel like a life sentence – if you're depressed, you're always going to be depressed," Flynne said.

Awareness of mental health issues is high, as is understanding and appreciation of how it can affect you. But there remains a disconnect between students' recognition of health problems and their willingness to actually go and do something about it.

Four out of five Australian teenagers think people their own age may not seek support for depression or anxiety because they're afraid of what others will think of them[33].

"Young people still feel ashamed of their feelings [in spite of efforts to reduce stigma in high schools], and they're reluctant to admit to their peers, their family, and particularly their school, that they're struggling. I've seen that in many of my friends who experience severe anxiety in high school," said Sophia.

Sam C. agreed, noting how his own struggles impacted upon his friendships. "We're bombarded with suicide statistics, but we often forget about the huge number of people that suffer in silence, and go about their daily business as if nothing were wrong, out of stigmatised fear," he said.

> "The stigmatised nature of mental illness ruined a number of my early high school relationships because, being so young, many of my friends did not understand how I felt. Some of these relationships never recovered."

I can understand why you would be fearful of telling your friends about struggles you're facing.

High school is a time in which fitting in with the group is crucial to your sense of self-worth and wellbeing. Any point of difference between you and others may be the line in the sand which means you're excluded.

As a result, those who do see the school counsellors, and run into each other in those offices, may feel like they have to hide it.

"There seemed to be the idea that you should be embarrassed about it, which is dumb," Holly M. said. "Serious mental health issues were to be kept to yourself and the professionals, as you risked being judged as weak or a freak if you saw someone about what you were going through."

But self-stigma can be just as damaging.

"There's almost this mentality of if you're not coping now [at school] then you won't cope at university. And you won't cope with a job. There's a spiral effect, and you think you'll end up on the street and probably die," Flynne said.

Overall, 36.9% of Aboriginal and Torres Strait Islander young persons are worried about discrimination – either lived experience or perceived – compared to just 24.9% of the rest of the youth population[34].

And it's not just mental health issues that you might feel the need to hide.

LGBTQI students may be impacted by a feeling of isolation, which can't be escaped.

"You feel or face exclusion, an inability to make or keep friends, which leads to isolation, anxiety, and fear of talking to people. It then impacts upon your performance at school, because you're feeling distracted by a secret that you're carrying," said Luke Furness, CEO of Out for Australia, an advocacy group supporting LGBTQI people in the workplace.

"It's a spiral – if you're worried about one thing, then you'll worry about another, and therefore you decide you won't go to a party with everyone else, which isolates you even further through self-selection of what you go to and whom you're willing to hang out with."

Whether you are a LGBTQI student or not, high school is about developing confidence to carry yourself in the real world. If that development is stunted – by your environment or by yourself – it has the potential to carry through in your life.

"We all get stressed, and therefore a bit of anxiety should be accepted as a normal part of everyone's life, as it occurs and impacts to varying degrees. As such, it should be openly talked about," said Debbie.

But … even though there is stigma in society that we can't always escape … there is still reason for you to have hope.

Think about your friendship circle, your family, your teachers and mentors. How many of them would think less of you as a person just because you're stressed or anxious? And, even if a couple of them did, how many would then use it as a weapon against you?

"None of [the students I tutor] have said, 'one of my friends has depression – what a pansy', or, 'my friend has anxiety attacks … what a bitch, she's using it as an excuse'. Never anything like that. It's always been, 'Oh yeah,

I know what that is, but what do I do with it?'" Camellia said.

This is where we come to the core issue of stigma.

Unlike other illnesses or injuries, there are no direct physical signs that you might be suffering from psychological distress, anxiety or depression (unless, of course, you have been self-harming).

Having bags under your eyes shows that you're tired, but might not make people realise that you're having anxiety attacks at night.

Losing weight may make people assume you're on a diet, rather than thinking you are suffering from an eating disorder.

Mental health issues are not like having a broken arm, where you can physically recognise and understand what the problem is. They are beneath the surface, making it harder for us to appreciate, and therefore more difficult for others to grasp as well.

In short: if people don't realise, they don't understand. Even if we are more aware of mental health issues, we are not necessarily more attuned to how we can look after ourselves and those around us. This creates fear. And fear leads to stigma.

But mental illnesses are no different to any other illnesses or injuries. They still require treatment. You would not ignore the flu or chicken pox. Don't ignore anxiety, depression and other mental ailments. Pushing them to one side only makes things worse.

"Healing and getting better starts with being real, and saying, 'I'm experiencing something'. When you're real and authentic, and are also supported and worthy of love from your parents, your best mate, and others around you, that takes away so much pain," Mitch Wallis said.

Don't suffer in silence. Don't fall victim to society's assumptions that suffering from stress, anxiety or depression – no matter how big or small – is somehow shameful or something to hide. Keeping things to yourself will only make matters worse.

TWD WELLBEING WISDOM

"Expressing how you are feeling helps others to understand your world. It's normal to experience the full range of positive and negative emotions," Dr Jenny Brockis said.

Suffering from anxiety or depression, on any level, is traumatic. Feeling like you can't talk to anyone about it, for fear of punishment or ridicule, makes things even worse. But you should not be fearful … here are a few reasons why:

- **Stigma often arises from not knowing how to respond**. Learn how you can look after yourself to manage stress and anxiety. Use the chapters throughout this book as a guide for the different issues you will face.

- **Disclosure does not have to be black and white**. While there will be some people whom you need to be wary of talking to, there are friends and family members whom you can trust. You do not have to suffer alone, and speaking up does not mean negative consequences if you pick the right audience.

- **Speaking up shows strength, not weakness**. Just as suffering from mental illness is not a sign of weakness, talking about it does not make you a different person to what you were yesterday. In fact, having the courage to speak about what you're going through is actually a sign of strength, because it shows you are willing to take steps to get better.

- **Everyone suffers to some extent**. There's not a person on Earth who doesn't feel stressed or anxious at some point. Whether you have a diagnosable condition is all just a matter of degrees. As such, you are not alone, and therefore, you are not unusual or weak in any way.

- **Self-stigma is self-defeating**. Getting down on yourself because of struggles in your life will only make those struggles worse. Reinforcing them by thinking of yourself as weak, or stupid, will only increase your anxiety and stress levels.

- **You are loved and cared for**. Your parents, siblings, mates and teachers are not going to think any less of you just because you are struggling. They have your back, and want to see you get better.

Juggling and managing your workload

"The volume of work was almost dangerous, leading many students to feel completely overwhelmed and that they had to work all the time," Holly M. said. "Some fell asleep in class because they had been up all night doing homework."

She summed up the students' response to the workload as follows: some swam, some trod water, and some drowned.

Looking back on those senior years of high school, I'd say I found myself in all three scenarios. I never drowned to the point of being unable to resurface, but there were certainly times where the amount of study required was too much, and I just wanted to give up and cry.

At the other end of the spectrum, sometimes I thrived under the pressure. There were days when I would operate so effortlessly that I felt I'd get through final exams without breaking a sweat.

> "Senior school workloads are incredibly tough," Sam C. said. "Not because it's unrealistically difficult, but just because there's so much of it. I found the transition to senior years to be pretty hard."

More often than not, however, Holly's feelings of treading water resonated with me.

You'd work so hard just to make it through to the end of the day without incident and distraction from your carefully considered (and colour-coordinated) timetable that even just reaching bedtime was a relief. Navigating those days was like always having to put out spot fires: just survive and push forward.

My mum often said when I was in Year 12 that the workload was much heavier than what she had at university in England in the late 1970s. I can only take her word for it. All I know is that it was far more than I wanted!

Navigating study requirements and the workload in the senior years of high school is the second greatest concern for young Australians between the ages of 15 and 19, trailing only concerns about stress. Almost 60% who are at risk of a mental illness list study and workload as being a serious worry[35]. Even among those not at risk of depression, over 31% say schooling commitments cause headaches that otherwise wouldn't exist[36].

But for both sexes, the workload is such that, as Milly put it, you feel constantly under pressure and your mind is always on homework and study.

"Home is no longer a sanctuary where you can relax and be yourself and do the things that you enjoy," she said. "It becomes another arena for you to stress and think about the amount of work you have to do in order to get a certain ATAR, and go to a certain university and do a certain course … your mind is always thinking about that pressure."

Teenage girls are more worried about study and workload issues than the boys. Sixty-five per cent of females in this age demographic who are at risk of mental illnesses say they are hugely concerned with study and workload, compared to just 48% of males[37].

The workload also comes at an inconvenient time.

"We are at an age where we are still developing physically and emotionally, and there's lots of pressures that aren't related to school to deal with too, like relationships, learning to drive, part-time jobs, extra-curricular activities, a social life, and learning who we are and want to be," Chelsea said. "Each teacher tells you to study for their subject at least an hour a night – that's not physically possible."

The other danger with having such a heavy workload is burnout. Your body and mind are not built to be pushed too hard for too long … eventually, you need a break.

Think about your family car … it requires a mechanical service every six months to ensure that everything is still running smoothly. You, as a person, require such "servicing" on a regular basis too.

You must find a balance in your daily and weekly schedule, and learn how to make time for both your homework and study as well as other activities, such as exercise and friendships.

It can be easy – and it is certainly tempting – to push all of those other commitments down to the bottom of your "to do" list when you are busy with school work, or have looming exams … but, it is still important that you make time for them.

There is more to life than school. Attending to other areas of your life will allow you to be your best, most energised and happy self, so that you can continue to focus in class, complete and take pride in your assignments, and overall, excel in school.[38]

TWD WELLBEING WISDOM

Unfortunately, you can't control the amount of work that you have on your plate (except in Years 11 and 12, where you can choose as many units of study as you want, so long as you meet your State's requirements).

In response, there are a few things you can do to ensure you're on top of both the workload and your wellbeing.

- **Pace yourself**. High school is a marathon, not a sprint. Work hard when you need to, have fun when you're allowed to, and always maintain a healthy balance.

- **Set a good routine**. In addition to having your school timetable, set a timetable for the hours before and after school in which you can fit in both specific study sessions and the things you want to be doing. Ensuring you know exactly when you're doing particular work, and then taking a break from it, helps you feel calmer and more organised.

- **Seek help where you need it**. Never be afraid to ask for assistance from your parents, teachers, friends or mentors … those people who love and care for you will always have your back.

- **Get your parents and friends to help you stay focused**. Use the people in your life to help you stay on track … whether it be through joint activities and events, or having them motivate and remind you about the importance of balance, it can only help to have your trusted confidants pushing you to achieve.

- **Remember, keeping a balance will not add to your workload**. Doing activities for your wellbeing, such as exercise, actually makes you more energised and motivated, rather than taking time away from the books.

- **Be proactive, not reactive!** It is always better to be prepared for issues before they arise, especially given how much homework and study you have to do. Get into good habits from the start, and you'll be ready to face any issues that arise.

- **Take individual responsibility**. While seeking support from others is crucial, nobody knows you better than yourself, and therefore you are best placed to figure out what will work and not work for you. Listen to your body and mind, and arrange your schedule to manage both the workload and your wellbeing.

- **Remember to manage your stable table-top**. As we discussed in an earlier chapter, conceptualise how you monitor your health and wellbeing. For me, it's a table-top with each leg representing a different aspect of my life. Always be mindful of your own table and how you're keeping it balanced and stable.

Why you shouldn't compete against others

"Not only do these kids feel like they need to be cool, they also have to be smart, and aiming to go to the best law school, or medical school, and on top of that they have to aim to be wealthy, and equitable, and egalitarian."

I went to a very high-achieving school. I was part of a group that was the high-achieving cohort when it came to academics, music, theatre, leadership positions, and especially sport.

On reflection, I did well. I made the 1st XI cricket team, had multiple colours for athletics, and was a school prefect. I was always near the top of the class in most subjects (maths and science being stark exceptions) and was, I think, well liked by my teachers and mates.

But I was never the best at any one thing. And it ate away at me.

Twelve years on, I know I'm lucky. But back then I was intensely jealous of others, including close friends, as I wanted to be number one.

This competitive streak followed me to law school, where it gained momentum, driving me to be a perfectionist and pushing me physically and emotionally to the limit, until I ultimately couldn't push myself any further.

My mental breakdown at the end of 2011 was partly due to my subconscious need to make everything a competition, never be satisfied with what I had done, and always compare myself to others.

By falling victim to this unhealthy competitive drive, I inadvertently left myself open to greater levels of stress, anxiety and, eventually, depression.

It is not possible, and certainly not sustainable, to be number one at everything you do. You have to manage your expectations of yourself, and appreciate your achievements for what they are, so that if and when you fail, you see it not as the end of the world, but as an opportunity to learn.

Lisa Farrow explained that pressure to perform comes from all angles – home, school, and from within.

"They feel a real need to achieve yet sometimes they want to achieve more than their current ability will enable them to.

That discrepancy causes them a lot of distress," she said.

"Within the adolescent population, it's all about comparison. Students compare themselves with their friends, especially with those who are really strong academically, and it causes them a lot of stress. They want to be as academically smart as those around them."

With social media and technology, it's much easier for you to see what others are doing and achieving, and then draw parallels between your life and theirs.

"Not only do these kids feel like they need to be cool, they also have to be smart, and aiming to go to the best law school, or medical school. On top of that they want to be wealthy, and equitable, and egalitarian," says Camellia, a Sydney-based high school tutor.

"The present climate is always giving you a reason to say you're not good enough," said Steve Zolezzi, a parent and educational psychologist in New South Wales.

"Progress will be made when individuals rely upon their own sense of self-worth, rather than being measured against the tribe or the team or social media."

Just as it did for me, competitiveness can arise even among close friends.

"I had three best friends in high school, and we were all very academically capable and also competitive. And that competitiveness was, I think, toxic for our friendships," Sophia said.

> "I wanted to be top of the class. I wanted to be doing well. And it caused me a lot of stress and additional pressure, because the marks supposedly mattered so much."

"School isn't life or death, but I did feel like both we and the school put completely unrealistic pressure on grades and the ATAR," said Chelsea. "Competitiveness with marks was insane … I absolutely hated that aspect of [my school]. It was awful."

Competitiveness can pop up in unexpected places, fuelled by your friends and classmates.

"You might get a Snapchat from someone studying, showing you how many notes they've written, and you immediately think, 'I'm not prepared'," said Milly.

And while you might start feeling competitive if you receive such a Snap from your friends, it shows the sender is experiencing anxiety too. Showing off can be a way to feel better about how you're actually feeling … just as posting a hot photo of yourself and receiving compliments might give you an ego boost.

But the fear of looking weak has the potential to affect our personal relationships and our health and wellbeing.

"The biggest thing for any kid is the peer pressure of not wanting to be seen to be weaker, or lesser, or not as cool, or not as polished as the other kids," said Peter, a Sydney-based parent. "If you're not coping, or seen to not be coping, it can be devastating."

"If you don't get school captain, or make the sports team, that is absolutely part of being a human being. It doesn't reflect who you are in life," Mitch Wallis said.

There's nothing wrong with being competitive. We're all products of the environment in which we grow up. And while competitiveness – even at unhealthy levels – is not your fault, it is still important to address it.

Firstly, try to be more introspective about your progress, and don't get bogged down by what others are doing. You can only reasonably compare yourself to yourself, anyway, as everybody is running their own race and you have no influence or control over anyone else.

Secondly, try to be comfortable in your own skin and okay with the fact that you are human, and simply cannot be the best at everything you do. Develop self-awareness of who you are, what you are good at and where you can succeed. This will allow you to better dedicate time and energy to that which truly matters, rather than simply competing against others for the sake of looking and feeling strong.

And thirdly, talk openly with friends, family and mentors about how you're feeling. Discussing your thoughts honestly will help you gain insight and perspective.

TWD WELLBEING WISDOM

- **Run your own race**. You can only control what you do you, not what others do. So there's no use in worrying about your classmates and friends ... just focus on your own efforts.

- **Learn to be okay with not always being number one**. Embrace occasional disappointing performance, or even failure. It happens to all of us, and is not a reflection on your abilities should you stumble here and there.

- **Share rather than compete**. Given the workload in the senior years of high school, it can be useful to split the burden of note taking. Form a study group for mutual benefit rather than competition.

- **Talk openly with friends and classmates**. Discussing how you feel about different subjects or activities will help you realise that those around you experience the same anxiety about performance – you are not alone.

- **Learn from mentors**. Even the most successful people in your life, whom you look up to and admire, have suffered and failed. Hearing about how they responded to such times, and learned from their experiences, will help you manage.

Maintaining a healthy body and diet

Seventy per cent of teenage girls are dissatisfied with their bodies[39]. Further, it is assumed that about 20% of teenage girls in Australia have undiagnosed eating disorders[40].

I was a skinny kid growing up. And my schoolmates made sure I knew it.

I never felt bullied by them but I do remember feeling physically inadequate in comparison to these guys, most of whom played rugby (one of whom went on to play for the Wallabies).

Remembering what it was like to be skinny at high school, who was never allowed to play rugby because my parents feared I'd get snapped in half, motivated me to take strength and fitness seriously in my adult life. These days I hit the gym roughly three times each week to lift weights. This is good for my physical and mental health, but I'm also vain and don't want to be seen as skinny! I want to be seen as strong and, ultimately, attractive to women (come at me, ladies).

Most of this is in my head, of course.

We are all our own worst critics, and anyone close to me would probably tell me I look great if I were to express concern about my appearance. And deep down, I sometimes agree with them – I'll admit that I don't look like a troll.

But it's hard to shake the feeling that you don't look good enough, both for yourself and those around you.

> "Having body image concerns as a young person can lead to negative feelings [about yourself as a whole], which can lead to anxiety and depression, which can then lead to eating problems or even disorders," said Professor Lina Ricciardelli.

SIGNS AND SYMPTOMS: You should seek immediate help, both from your parents and medical professionals, if you are suffering from any of the following signs and symptoms[41] of disorders such as anorexia nervosa or bulimia nervosa:

PHYSICAL WARNING SIGNS

- Rapid weight loss, frequent changes in weight, loss of or disturbance in menstrual cycle, fainting, dizziness, constant fatigue, not sleeping well, bodily swelling, feeling cold all the time.

PSYCHOLOGICAL WARNING SIGNS

- Preoccupation with eating, food and weight, feeling anxious at meal time, feeling "out of control", having a distorted body image, being obsessed with shape and size, using food as comfort or punishment.

BEHAVIOURAL WARNING SIGNS

- Eating in private, avoiding meal times with others, vomiting, hoarding of food, change in clothing style, compulsive exercising, making lists of good or bad foods, sudden dislike of foods you have always enjoyed, extreme sensitivity about body shape, weight and size, and being secretive about food.

BODY IMAGE

Many high school students, boys and girls like you, also feel like they don't look good enough.

> Thirty-six per cent of boys at risk of mental health issues see body image as a serious concern, and for girls the rates are even more alarming: 65.9% are very concerned with how they look. That means in a co-ed class of 10 students, 5 will be worried about how they look to an extent that impacts their wellbeing[42].

Boys and girls have different concerns when it comes to their bodies.

Of those worried about how they look, boys tend to be focused on being bigger and more muscular[43], whereas girls try to lose weight and conform with ideals of being thin[44].

"Boys tend to focus more on the positive aspects of their body image and in particular the functional aspects but, in saying that, many boys are concerned with being more muscular, being bigger, faster, and better on the sports field," said Professor Ricciardelli. "With girls, it's still primarily wanting to lose weight and to have the thin ideal. More girls want to be more toned as well and have more muscular definition, so it's not just a focus by any means on wanting to just lose weight. Primarily, the concerns are more with desiring the thin ideal."

There are, of course, many social and cultural factors that pressure us to be a certain way, and for girls in particular, the media often portrays a very particular image for how you should look[45].

With everything we see in popular culture about ideal body types – how much kale and coconut oil you're supposed to eat, for example – we've reached a point where almost everyone questions how they look, and no one feels comfortable anymore.

When asked about the female students in her care, Lisa Farrow said, "We don't often have students coming to us and saying, 'I really hate the way I look', because I think it's now just considered to be the norm; it's almost expected that you would think in this way."

In 2016, 55% of young persons aged 15–19 who screened as having a probable mental illness said they were very or extremely concerned about body image. Among those who had no probable mental illness, the figures were still very high, at 24%[46].

Nobody is perfect. All of us would change something about our appearance, given the chance.

But getting hung up on what percentage of body fat you have, or whether or not you have a suitable "bikini bridge" or "box gap" for Instagram photos, not only distracts you from more important things in life, it also makes you more susceptible to eating disorders.

What we need to do is focus on positivity.

"Positive reinforcement, and social support, have been shown to be important in getting young people to feel connected to their bodies and feel greater acceptance," said Professor Ricciardelli.

EATING DISORDERS

"What's so hard for someone going through an eating disorder is that people might not understand the rationale, which makes them (the person suffering) feel worse. So, not only are they potentially feeling conscious about the way they look), but they're also wondering 'why doesn't anyone else know why I feel that way?'. If we stop and listen to what someone is going through, instead of judging them, we can provide them with the support they are really looking for: to be seen, accepted & loved unconditionally," Mitch Wallis said.

Despite being incredibly rare, being killed by a crocodile remains one of the scariest and most notorious ways someone can die in Australia. Crocs don't just rip you apart … they hold onto you, stifle you, drown you with a roll technique, or – if that doesn't work – they starve you and leave you to die a slow, painful death then wait until your body rots to a soft pulp until finally eating you (fun fact: crocodiles can't chew … hence why they might wait to actually eat you).

Eating disorders like anorexia are like crocodiles.

They sneak up on you, wrap their arms around your shoulder with the promise of making you thinner, or bigger, or stronger, and – before you know it – they've overwhelmed you to the point of no return.

Teenagers are especially at risk of eating disorders – they are the second leading cause of mental illnesses for young females[47].

Despite what some people think, eating disorders are not solely suffered by white, middle-class women. Eating disorders do not discriminate, and can affect men and women alike, and all socioeconomic and cultural backgrounds.

Nor are they just about food, or being vain and self-interested, or going too far with a particular diet. And while they are not as well-known – and therefore understood – as mental illnesses such as depression, they are, in fact, just as deadly.

Eating disorders are driven by emotions. They begin with thoughts about weight, dieting, control or exercise, and then develop into anxieties such as guilt, obsession and a sense of spiralling out of control.

Binge eating disorder affects 47% of the Australian population[48], and presents itself as a way of dealing with negative or difficult emotions, such as elevated distress, anxiety or depression. Sufferers often eat alone and feel ashamed of the amount they've had and feeling so out of control[49].

What is most troubling is that teenage eating disorders are on the rise. Between 1995 and 2005, the rates of both males and females over the age of 15 who screened positive for eating disorders *doubled*[50].

People who have an eating disorder suffer from a type of depression, regardless of their weight and size[51]. But eating disorders don't always come from dissatisfaction with body image, weight or size. They can also be caused by mental illnesses themselves, such as depression.

Disorders such as anorexia nervosa and bulimia nervosa affect approximately 9% of the Australian population, and around 15% of women and girls.

"We need to take the focus away from just body image, making sure kids develop well-rounded lives," Professor Ricciardelli said. "It is important to fit in with your peers, to fit in society, but it shouldn't dominate our lives."

Just like anxiety, depression and suicidal thoughts – there is always a way out of an eating disorder. You can recover … but you have to seek help.

On the next page, you'll find some tips, and in the Resources chapter you'll find some hotlines, websites and apps as well.

TWD WELLBEING WISDOM

"A lot of eating disorders come from a need or want for control. So allowing ourselves to listen and find out what it is that we're trying to get control of will allow us to then realise where and why we need help," Mitch Wallis said.

If you are unhappy with your body image, remember[52] [53]:

- **Treat your body well**. Do things in moderation … don't exercise too hard or go on crazy diets … take it easy.

- **Don't try to be someone else**. Don't try to change who you are. You don't need to change for anyone. If any of your friends don't like you for who you are, then they're not worth hanging out with.

- **Focus on the parts of yourself that you like**. Everyone likes something about themselves. Focus on those things if you're ever feeling down about yourself. There are lots of things to love about you.

- **Remember that people online, on TV, in movies and magazines don't actually look like that**. They get airbrushed, photoshopped and digitally enhanced more than you could ever do with an Instagram filter. They look just like us.

- **Go easy on yourself, and your mates!** You probably treat your friends well, and wouldn't try to make them feel bad about how they look. So why not treat yourself the same way? Support yourself just as you would support and not tease or bully your friends.

- **You are much more than how you look**. Don't let your appearance dictate your life. Focus your energy and attention on things you're good at, your family and friends, so you can ensure your life as a teenager is fun and meaningful.

If you are suffering from an eating disorder, please[54]:

- **Do not feel ashamed**. Illness is never your fault. You wouldn't blame yourself for getting a cold … this is no different.

- **Be honest and brave**. The first step towards recovery is acknowledging you need help. It's a scary step to take, but it's also the bravest one. Options for support are listed in the Resources chapter.

- **Reach out**. No matter how you may feel, you are not alone. Talk to close friends and family members about what you're going through … they're there to help.

- **Be open about your feelings**. How you feel will vary from day to day (even hour to hour). Be transparent and up front with the people in your life. See the Communication chapter for more information.

- **Relapsing does not mean you are failing.** I still have days where I feel depressed, even though I've been out of the woods for about four years. You're allowed to have your off days. Eating disorders can re-emerge at times when you feel particularly vulnerable. Relapse is a normal part of the journey; believe that you can get back on track.

- **Know your trigger points.** It's important to know what makes you tick, as this knowledge can help you prevent making an illness worse. You can learn more about trigger points in the #triggered chapter.

- **Be patient.** Illness doesn't go away overnight. You can't put a date on when you will feel better, and trying to do it all at once will only make you feel more frustrated and anxious. Don't give up. Allow things to move at their own pace.

- **Reconnect with your healthy self.** There will be a part of you that does want to get better, even if your illness is telling you otherwise. Get in touch with your "healthy self" as often as you can. Medical professionals or counsellors can help you with this.

- **Be kind to yourself.** Being unwell doesn't mean you're weak. Take time out to rest and relax. Doing things that make you feel better is important.

Family feud: advice for you and your parents

"One girl in my class had it in her head that if she didn't get into a law degree, she couldn't live under her parents' roof anymore. Her whole final year was consumed by massive stress where she didn't want to do law, but said, 'If I don't get into law, then I'm basically disowned.'"

Parents want the best for their kids. We are all born helpless and unable to fend for ourselves, and our parents have a natural inclination to do all they can for us. If and when we are struggling, our parents can offer security that we cannot find anywhere else.

However, sometimes it's those very people who love us the most who can be the cause of our stress and anxiety.

This chapter looks at the ways in which your parents and guardians can negatively impact your health and wellbeing. It's important to realise it's borne out of love … but it's still good to be aware.

CHANGING DYNAMICS

As a teenager you are developing – physically, socially, emotionally and intellectually – and are becoming less and less reliant on your parents and family structure. This is normal. But while your parents can appreciate this logically, it can be hard for them to accept it.

Sam D., who was deputy principal of a Catholic boys' school in Sydney for 15 years, said teenagers get to a point where, "your parents don't do it for you anymore, and the hero-worship of the father figure gets replaced very, very quickly by the friendship group".

Such a changing dynamic, he said, leads to strain in relationships.

The same is true of girls. "They start to move away from their families [around Year 9], and their world is more focused on their peers. This can then cause conflict within the family as parents navigate their change in role," said Lisa Farrow.

"Parents have to let go, allow their kids to make mistakes, while being there to support them. It's the hardest thing, but you have to do it. The more a parent tries to hold on and hover and make solutions for children, force relationships and engagement, the more it won't work," Sam D. said.

This shift in dynamic sees you form your own sense of identity, which can be as frustrating a process as it is stressful.

"We used to see a lot of parents try to be more like mates with their children [once they reached this stage], but teenagers don't need that. They need parents," Sam D. said. "They don't need more friends – they've got more than enough. Some crucial parenting skills can get lost here, leading to dysfunction in the family."

Ultimately, parents need to let go and allow their kids to start making decisions and relying on themselves.

"HELICOPTER PARENTING"

While it can be challenging for your parents or guardians to watch you fail or wonder if you will succeed, as a teenager you need to be able to learn to do this in order to live a healthy, successful adult life.

Hovering "helicopter parents" can make you anxious. They can affect your emotional growth, and have longer-term detrimental effects on your development as an adult[55].

And while they might hover in a warm and loving way, you may still suffer lower self-worth, indulge in high-risk behaviours such as binge drinking, and be susceptible to increased levels of stress and anxiety[56].

Not only that, you might be less engaged at school, prone to depression and less satisfied with life in general. This is the opposite to what your hovering parents intended!

"If teenagers don't have the in-built resilience, or they haven't learned that resilience to push back, it is very difficult for them to respond," Camellia said.

> "Parenting pressures can be detrimental to a student's wellbeing, because if the parents put too much pressure on the student, they will – like most things under pressure – crack. I know I did," said Holly M.

"Our parents need to be aware that they need to relax on the academic pressure they're putting on their children because that can create a lot of stress and anxiety that isn't necessary," Sophia said.

"I think parents' intentions are good, and they really love their child, but they don't allow them to have the freedom and independence to make decisions, all part of what should be happening in life, and unfortunately it delays their development. In doing so, it puts the child under a lot of pressure," said Chris Gould, pastoral care director at a school in Sydney.

You will thrive, for example, if your parents are involved in the school community[57], even through something as simple as turning sausages at a school barbeque.

What is needed is balance, and – even if it goes against the instincts of your carers – to put your wellbeing first.

UNCONDITIONAL LOVE INDIRECTLY CREATING PERFORMANCE ANXIETY

Even when your parents or guardians are unconditionally supportive, you may still feel under pressure.

> "I went to a private school. I saw, over the years, what [my parents] sacrificed. I almost felt as though I owed it to them to do the very best that I could … I pushed myself to the limits to do that," Flynne said.

This is a scenario that I can relate to, but in a slightly different way. I was never told to study harder. My parents gave me and my siblings leeway when it came to household chores at times when we were under the pump. Mum and Dad recognised that Year 12 was the most important thing in our lives, and it would be helpful to us to not have to worry about more than we needed to.

But, through no fault of theirs, this bred a sense of

obligation within me to do the best I could. I was already driven and determined to do well, but the idea of letting down my parents added another layer of pressure.

This feeling has never really gone away. I still strive to make my parents proud.

What I sometimes forget, however, is that my parents love me – always have and always will. And as long as I am doing my best, they will be proud.

If your parents are like Flynne's, and mine, remember that, no matter what, in your parents' eyes, you will always be worthy of their love, care and support.

On the following pages I've listed some suggestions for parents and guardians to help them better support you during stressful times at school. Show this chapter to them.

There is one thing you can do to better manage your relationship when it becomes hard: communicate openly and respectfully.

Your parents or guardians are trying their best and want you to succeed. They want to know how they can help. Be up front and honest about what you need, about how what they say influences how you feel, and about what will make you feel more comfortable when things get tough.

TWD WELLBEING WISDOM

"We have to accept and love our children for who they are. Some may be high achievers, and some may not. That doesn't determine who they'll be as adults. We should avoid trying to make them into what they're not, because that's where you get animosity, it's where you get children feeling like they haven't lived up to your expectations and they're not who you want them to be," said Natalie, a Perth-based parent.

School can make us worried or upset and affect our academic performance and self-esteem. Issues at home often make those worries even worse.

Here are some suggestions for your parents or guardians[58] to help you manage the rigours of high school, stave off anxiety and better navigate your relationships:

- **Don't let your kids over-schedule themselves.** While it is important for teenagers to keep up with activities outside of school, it's also important for them to have time for relaxation and recuperation. Time for indulgence and guilty pleasures is important, too.

- **Make sure your kids get a good night's sleep.** This is just as important as making time for relaxation. As you'll see in the next chapter, even one extra hour of sleep per night can aid physical, emotional and psychological health and development.

- **Let kids play!** While it may be tempting to strap your kids to the desk and make sure they're studying, it is crucial that they also have time for fun – not just to unwind and de-stress, but for the sake of creativity and cognitive functioning.

- **Encourage kids to care for their physical health.** Exercise is crucial not only for our physical wellbeing, but also our emotional and psychological states. It is also a proven stress reliever and mood enhancer. Ensure that your kids are active, so that their study sessions are productive.

- **Lead by example.** If you want your kids to be managing their stress and wellbeing, you need to do the same. Eat well and exercise regularly, don't drink too much, switch off devices before bed … all the things you would suggest to your kids.

- **Help them develop good coping strategies.** Structure and organisation are fundamentally important to high school students whose schedules are already regimented by the school timetable. Collaborate with them to develop a week-long timetable that includes homework and study but also exercise, fun and relaxation.

- **Label negative emotions accordingly**. Understanding that stress and anxiety affects us all is beneficial in showing you're not alone, or weak. Labelling and talking about emotions, both good and bad, helps normalise them and lessen their impact on your child's wellbeing.

- **Teach them to focus on what they can control, not what they can't**. Just as we can't control the weather, your child has no influence over how well the student sitting next to them in class is doing. Helping them focus on their own progression and achievement will increase their confidence and capacity to cope with whatever comes their way.

- **Reassure them that everything will be okay**. No matter how hard things seem right now, life goes on. We aren't perfect, and we often need help. Your kids need to feel comfortable asking for help from you, their teachers and their friends. They need to know that asking for help is not a sign of weakness but an effective and positive coping strategy.

SLEEPING YOUR WAY TO THE TOP! (Part I):

How does lack of sleep affect my wellbeing?

A healthy, balanced diet is crucial to having a healthy body. In the same way, getting enough sleep is necessary to have a healthy mind. Sleep is nutrition for the brain. And if you're not feeding your brain, you're just not going to be productive.

Statistically, high school students are not getting enough sleep. Are you sacrificing sleep, and your success too?

I was able to maintain a pretty good sleep routine while at high school, but once I started at university, that went out the window.

In my final two years of my law and communications degrees, I survived on about four or five hours sleep a night. I put it down to the heavy study load, working part-time as a paralegal in a commercial law firm, and volunteering 30–35 hours a week. This schedule was ultimately too much. My breakdown in late 2011 was caused by a number of factors, but lack of sleep was definitely one of them.

Being tired over a long period of time caused larger issues; by not taking proper care of myself, I wasn't able to function effectively or be as productive as I wanted. As a result, my stress and anxiety levels increased to the point that, when I realised I had depression, I had no idea of what was "normal" or "healthy"[59].

In the American state of Virginia, only 3% of students report getting the recommended nine hours of sleep per night, with 20% saying they slept five hours or less. Each hour of lost sleep led to a 38% increase in the odds of feeling sad or hopeless; a 23% increase in substance abuse; a

42% increase in thoughts of suicide; and a 58% increase in actual suicide attempts[60].

Even just one extra hour of sleep can make the world of difference. As that US study showed, just an extra 60 minutes could save you from all sorts of destructive scenarios[61].

Don't blame yourself for always feeling tired. When you're a teenager, there's a delay in the release of the sleep hormone melatonin from our brains to our bodies. As a result, you're often not tired until later at night, compared to young kids and adults[62].

As a teenager, you need around nine hours of sleep each night. But given that you're not able to fall asleep until later, and still have to get up early to go to school, you might be constantly falling short of the recommended number of hours needed.

This not only makes it harder to get up in the morning, but it can also make you physically unwell, irritable, prone to mood swings, anxiety and depression, and reduce your ability to concentrate[63].

"For adolescents, a natural sleeping pattern would be to

stay up late and then sleep late. Unfortunately, the design of our school system makes them get up really early, when their brains want to be sleeping, and we make them go to bed earlier than they want to," said Lisa Farrow. "Girls at our school are not able to go to bed early. A normal bedtime is 11.00 pm, and while we know that they need a minimum of nine or 10 hours of sleep at that age for optimal functioning, on average they're getting six or seven hours."

Not getting enough sleep can cause you to overeat the next day. Your body will crave those extra calories as a reward for not resting[64]. In short ... better sleep will help you keep off unwanted weight.

I know you're incredibly busy: you've got class all day, homework at night, part-time jobs or babysitting gigs, extra-curricular stuff like sport, music or drama, and social lives. Often, it feels like there just aren't enough hours in the day to do everything.

But you've got to do a few things to help yourself get to sleep, too.

With the proliferation of mobile phones and laptops, it's easy to stay up late, but this affects not only the quality of your sleep but also how well you function the next day.

Dr Jenny Brockis said humans aren't designed to be connected to a screen, or be on devices, all day long. It hyper-stimulates the brain and decreases our chances of being able to switch off and relax.

"Our screens emit a light that interferes with melatonin production needed to prepare us for sleep. While you can switch to a yellow background at night, staying online continues to stimulate neuronal activity adding," she said. "Everyone benefits from switching off all technology 60–90 minutes before bed to allow the brain the time it needs to quieten down."

With smartphones and tablets hosting all of your social media channels as well as the Internet, and Netflix, you can be forgiven for wanting to be connected all the time.

But we also need to have some downtime before bed, so that we can tell our bodies, both physically and psychologically, that it's time to recharge so we can be at our best the following day.

> Teens who use their phones after lights out tend to sleep worse than others, which leads to poorer mental health, lower self-esteem and more behavioural problems[65].

Part of the problem is that we love having our phones next to our beds or on our bedside tables. It's so easy to reach over while we're under the covers and grab our device. I admit that I'm terrible at this. I often reach for my phone after having gone to bed … it's just so easy to do. But the stats are clear: excess screentime before bed makes it harder to fall asleep and that has all sorts of knock-on effects. Your alarm clock is still going to go off at the same time, no matter what you do!

While a lack of sleep is detrimental to our health, getting a good night's sleep can give us the boost we need to study efficiently, eat and exercise better, and be successful.

Thankfully, there are plenty of tools available to help us not only fall asleep, but make sure we're getting quality sleep. When it comes to your health and wellbeing, you *can* sleep your way to the top (metaphorically, of course). You can read more about how to get good sleep in the second half of this chapter.

SLEEPING YOUR WAY TO THE TOP! (Part II):

How can good sleep improve my wellbeing?

"Sleep is one of the foundations of wellbeing, and if we don't have that in place, then our health can never really be at 100%," said Pree Benton.

Here are a number of strategies to help you get better sleep, improve your wellbeing and make you more productive and successful. You can, metaphorically, sleep your way to the top!

MAKE SLEEP A NON-NEGOTIABLE PART OF YOUR ROUTINE

> "If your sleep isn't optimal, then everything else is going to be more difficult to manage. Make sure you're getting good sleep – just as you need to be exercising regularly and eating a well-balanced diet. If those things are out of balance, your mental health is going to suffer," said Lisa Farrow.

A lack of sleep contributed to the breakdown that kick-started my 18-month struggle with anxiety and depression. Catching up on lost sleep, and subsequently making sleep a non-negotiable aspect of my life, has helped me get things back on track. Sleep is an integral part of my daily schedule. It helps me function better and feel whole.

"Sleep is one of the foundations of wellbeing, and if we don't have that in place, then our health can never really be at 100%," said Pree Benton.

Don't skimp on sleep! You'll be much more refreshed, and therefore productive, if you allow yourself to properly rest and recharge your batteries.

GET INTO A GOOD ROUTINE, AND STICK TO IT

"One of my friends didn't really care about sleep, and as a result he was always so tired, and his friends were the same ... they'd be sleeping in class, and that's not really beneficial. I always really cared about my sleep and getting the recommended number of hours," said Alicia (not her real name), who attended a private girls' school in Sydney.

> "I always make sure I'm not studying past 10.30 pm. I know it works for some people to be up until 2.00 am, as they feel like they're not allowed to stop studying until the work is finished. But I need to get my sleep. I don't compromise on that," said Flynne.

Sleep is already enough of a wellness issue for teenagers without us messing with our internal body clocks. Staying up later to finish off assignments, or even just because we want to, wreaks havoc on your body.

The same goes for sleeping in too late on the weekends. You may feel the need to "catch up" but that will just keep you up later the next night, which throws you for a further loop.

Set times to both fall asleep and then wake up the following morning, and – wherever possible – don't deviate from them. Predictability and routine will be your best friends in ensuring that you can function at the level you need the following day.

DON'T DO AN ALL-NIGHTER ... EVER

"Sleep deprivation does not work – and it doesn't take a neuroscientist to figure that out," Sam C. said.

> "Do not pull all-nighters, because you're only screwing your own ATAR. Do not sabotage your health on the logic that you think it's benefiting your academic performance – it's not."

If you mess with your sleeping patterns by pulling an all-nighter, your whole cycle is thrown out the window.

Students may see an all-night study session as being a time-effective way to cram for an exam, or complete an assignment, but in reality, it both affects your wellbeing and productivity, and is a terrible way to learn and retain info. Better time management will always get you better results.

EARN YOUR SLEEP

"The only way to metabolise cortisol from your system is to undergo strenuous aerobic exercise. The test is if you were walking you have to walk fast enough that you couldn't hold a conversation. You would be out of breath if you were to try and start to talk. That's my number one thing [for better sleep], because you have to get that chemical out of you or get it back to a normal level in order to deal with the stress and sleep problems," advised Camellia.

> Simply put, it is much easier to fall asleep if you are physically tired. Incorporate exercise into your daily routine so that your body and brain are better equipped to switch off at the end of the day.

I always sleep better on days when I have been active, compared to days where I have just sat at my desk or been lying on the couch. If we are inactive, it is much harder for our bodies to tell when we are supposed to be awake or asleep. Force your body to recognise the difference by earning your sleep!

TURN OFF ALL DEVICES 30–60 MINUTES BEFORE BED

"I sleep with my phone next to my bed, but I don't touch it within 30 minutes of going to sleep. Instead, I read," Sam C. said.

I read every night before going to sleep. Detaching from my laptop and phone, and having time at the end of the day to do something calming (such as reading a book) helps me not only relax my eyes, but also provides a psychological reminder that it's time to wind down.

LISTENING TO ESCAPE

"Listening to audiobooks can help you get out of your own head and stop thinking about whatever might be stressing you out or making you anxious," said Milly.

This might not be for everyone but, sometimes, it can be soothing to listen to something to help you drift off to sleep. Avoid death metal and news and politics ... try audiobooks and classical music instead. Listening to mindful meditation podcasts might also be of use ... I write more about this later in the book.

CHANGE THE SETTINGS ON YOUR PHONE

If you really can't disconnect from your device, then at least make them such that the brightness, or blue light, does as little damage to your ability to relax and fall asleep.

Depending on what sort of phone you have, it should be easy to fiddle with the settings to change the brightness or colour schemes. There are even apps available that can help you do this too.

"Within an hour of going to sleep, I change the display settings on the phone to emit less blue light, which helps prepare my body to wind down," Sam C. said.

Little tricks like this – even if the difference made is only trivial – will make it easier for you to fall asleep. So why not give it a try?

TWD WELLBEING WISDOM

- **Make sleep a non-negotiable part of your routine**. Sleep is one of the key aspects of your health and wellbeing. Don't ignore your need for rest … it has flow-on effects.

- **Don't sleep in for too long on the weekends in an effort to catch up**. This will only make your body less tired at night time, keeping you up even later, resulting in more hours of lost sleep.[66]

- **Keep a regular sleeping pattern**, with a routine bedtime each night so you have a constant rhythm.[67]

- **Don't do all-nighters.** Aside from the havoc it will wreak upon your normal routine, it won't help you produce quality work or retain more info.

- **Earn your sleep**. Try to exercise each day so that you feel like you've earned your sleep. Don't exercise too close to bedtime, however.

- **Switch off your devices long before bed**. Avoid using devices such as your phone and laptop at least 60 minutes before bed, so your brain can start to unwind and you are able to fall asleep quicker.

- **Change the settings on your phone**. You can adjust the brightness on your phone – or even use apps to change its colouring – in order to ease the strain on your eyes. If phone use gives you headaches, or makes you stay up later, do whatever you can to ease that strain.

- **Listen**. Tune in to something relaxing, such as soothing music or an audiobook of one of your favourite novels. But don't do this one if it means you have to concentrate too hard.

- **Be wise about diet.** Try not to eat too much food or drink before bedtime … especially stimulants like coffee or energy drinks which will disrupt your sleep and keep you awake.

Teens, tech and social media

I didn't get my first mobile phone until I was 16.

At the time, it was frustrating to have to wait so long. My mates all had phones at least a year or two before me. Mobiles had just started to really take off, with Nokia dominating the market (RIP *Snake* game).

When I was in my early 20s, I worked at my local primary school, looking after kids in the before and after school care programs. I was shocked to see so many children in Years 5 and 6 with mobiles. Fast-forward to today, and it is not uncommon to see young kids playing on iPads in restaurants.

But too much screen time is, unfortunately, now associated with physical, mental and social health concerns.

SOCIAL MEDIA

Many changes in society brought about by new technologies have been for the better; social networking sites have provided a way for teenagers to be more connected and have opportunities to learn from each other[68], as demonstrated by the numerous study blogs and note-sharing sites for high school students.

But social media platforms have also been detrimental for the health and wellbeing of society, particularly for younger people.

Facebook overuse, for example, can negatively impact your health and wellbeing. One study found that constant exposure can lower your self-esteem because of increased awareness of your own internal, social standards[69].

In other words, viewing someone else's profile leads you to compare yourself to the world around you.

Katie Bennett, a careers consultancy coach in the US, said this tendency to constantly compare ourselves to others online was detrimental to our sense of wellbeing.

"One of the biggest sources of insecurity is that we compare our behind-the-scenes lives to everyone else's highlights reel," she explained.

> "We see a glimpse of other people's lives on social media channels while we're sitting at home, doing something boring, and we feel inadequate. This is really dangerous, when you're comparing your whole life with that surface level portrayal of another person's life."

Sophia noted the pressure such highlights reels indirectly place upon students. "Instagram has, particularly for females, been difficult because it puts extra pressures on young people that they don't even need, like the supposed need to look good in a bikini or that you need to be going to 'x' number of school formals. I think it's important for parents to help set social media boundaries for their kids, because they can become consumed by this fake world."

Adults do this just as much as high school students. It's important to be aware of our tendency to compare ourselves to others, and not get bogged down if ever we feel upset about what we see others do online.

> Teenagers who spend large amounts of time on social media say they are less content, more likely to get into trouble, are often sad or unhappy, and – ironically – bored[70].

Facebook and Instagram can consume a lot of time, and while it might be fun for a while, ultimately they won't help with your homework or study – and more than likely they're going to negatively impact your health and wellbeing.

"Social media can become a bottomless pit of procrastination," Holly G. said. "Hours spent scrolling through Facebok or Instagram are hours you can't get back when you've got an exam tomorrow."

In 2011, 68% of teenage girls in the US reported having had a negative experience on a social networking site[71]. Some reported that Facebook can facilitate fights, especially through the creation of "burn" pages, created with the intention of taunting or teasing classmates[72].

Too much time spent on social media leads to less time for outdoor physical activities such as sport and exercise, as well as other pursuits such as reading, mindfulness or meditation.

It's simple: there are only so many hours in the day … and the more time we spend on social media, the less time we have for other things that may benefit our physical, emotional or psychological health.

TEXTING AND SEXTING

I'm sure you're responsible with your text messaging habits.

As you've no doubt found since having a mobile phone, or being able to chat to friends via Facebook Messenger, it's sometimes hard to gauge the reaction of the other person. It's hard to convey tone and emotion through such messages (the introduction of emojis has made this easier, but it's still not like chatting face-to-face).

I have, in the past, made mistakes with texts. I've written a (not so flattering) text about someone and, instead of sending it to a friend to bitch or gossip, I've sent it to the person about whom the message was written! I've also sent texts to intended recipients and then immediately regretted my tone or language.

Almost half of teenagers who own mobile phones say they have sent a text message that they later regretted[73].

Some kids send texts to bully or intimidate others and, in some cases, screengrabs of conversations will be uploaded to online platforms. You might have done this before, or perhaps you've been a victim of it.

Mobile phones, instant messaging services and social media platforms are also increasingly being used to monitor, threaten and harass.

One in three high school students who are in romantic relationships say that they've been texted by their partner multiple times to find out where they are, what they are doing or who they are with[74]. Students who find themselves on the receiving end of this are going to suffer adverse effects on their emotional and psychological wellbeing.

As many as 20% of teenagers in the US report having both sent and received nude or semi-nude images or videos of themselves[75]. Not only that, teenagers in relationships are finding themselves being pressured into sending such pictures, or flirty texts, by their partners. If they don't, they risk being publicly criticised[76].

I don't want to tell you that you shouldn't send your boyfriend or girlfriend photos of yourself. It's common practice for adults, and so why can't you do the same thing? And what does it have to do with your health and wellbeing?

Just imagine turning up to school naked because you forgot to put on your school uniform that morning. Other students would laugh at you, perhaps with a few teachers having a giggle too. It'd be embarrassing, shameful, and you might never live it down.

Now imagine that your naked body could be seen by those same classmates at any time, on any day, and not just that one time you forgot to put on clothes before going into school.

> While sexting is, in most cases, simply a way of engaging in an intimate fashion with your boyfriend or girlfriend, there is always the risk that the recipient will share them with someone else, or post them more broadly – particularly if that relationship breaks down.

You've probably heard of revenge porn: the practice of posting an ex-partner's private images or videos online in order to get back at them for something or other. It can result in trust issues, post-traumatic stress disorder, anxiety, depression and suicidal tendencies, among other mental health issues[77].

"A girl I met was telling me that all the boys in her class have different folders [on their phones] containing various girls' nude photos. If the girls were to get out of line, they'd threaten to send them as a revenge porn concept," Flynne said.

Social media and advancements in technological devices have truly revolutionised the ways in which we operate and communicate. This has been positive in many ways, but there are also inherent dangers that can affect your health and wellbeing. Be aware, be safe, be kind, and – most of all – be yourself.

TWD WELLBEING WISDOM

Using social media and playing with your phone and laptop is a lot of fun. Even for adults! But you do still need to bear some things in mind.

- **Remember that social media shows the highlights reel, not behind-the-scenes life**. Don't get caught up in what others are doing online … they may be posting about having a great time, but you never know what is truly going on, just as they might not know about your struggles.

- **Monitor your time spent online**. Social media use can help us feel more connected, but the more we use it, the more anxious and stressed we can also feel. Give yourself time limits each day.

- **Pick and choose times to use social media, so that you can study effectively**. Procrastination is the enemy of effective study. Allow yourself certain times of day to be online, then disconnect while you're getting your work done.

- **Don't use tech 30–60 minutes before bedtime**. As we discussed in the chapter on sleep, disconnect from all tech devices well before bed.

- **Be yourself**. Whether you're on social media or on your phone, don't be anyone other than who you are. Be true to your own personality and don't be swayed by others.

- **Be mindful of what you are posting and sending**. Remember that once a post is out there, it's almost impossible to take back. Be careful about what you're putting out into the world. A good test is: would you be embarrassed, or ashamed, if everyone you know saw what you posted or sent?

- **Treat others as you would want to be treated**. Be nice! Cyber-bullying, which we discuss in another chapter, has a significant impact upon our health and wellbeing.

- **Don't engage with strangers**. There are weirdos and whackos on every corner of the Internet. As a minor, you are especially vulnerable … communicate only with those people you know.

- **Keep all passwords to yourself**. Don't share your login details with anyone, not even friends or partners. You never know what someone else might do with your confidential information.

- **Last but not least … have fun**! The online sphere is an amazing place, which can open you up to so many new things. Use your tech freedom wisely.

Beating bullying, online and in person

"When you're being bullied at school, it's hard to see that life's ever going to be different."

Mental health issues such as anxiety and depression can be both a result of, and a reason for, being bullied[78]. That is, depression and severe suicide ideation are strongly linked to being bullied and can be a reason for being bullied or acting like a bully.

Gone are the days where high schools saw bullying as simply being "part of growing up". Thank goodness, because bullying is destructive and can have serious effects on your physical and emotional health and development.

Students who question their own sexual orientation are teased more, feel more depressed and subsequently use more drugs, compared to heterosexual teenagers, or even homosexual or bisexual students who know their sexual orientation[79].

The elevated risk of bullying, or discrimination, in turn increases the risk that LGBTQI students will suffer from mental health issues, or have suicidal tendencies[80] – on top of having to come to terms with a sexual orientation that may differ from the majority of their friends and peers.

There were 140 boys in my year at high school. None came out while we were students – including a couple of guys in my extended friendship group – and, in hindsight, it's easy to understand why.

Being an all-boys' school, any classmates whose personalities, physical traits or even voices gave the impression that they may have been gay, were teased. I'm confident the intentions of those doing the teasing wouldn't have been malicious … as young teenage boys, the majority of us wouldn't have had much understanding of LGBTQI issues.

But that doesn't change the fact that for those who were victims of teasing (and even for those watching on, seeing themselves in the victims), it must have been torturous.

Whether you're gay or straight, you need to know how to manage it if you're ever faced with a bully, either in the playground or online. And while both schools and parents need to protect students, there are plenty of things that we can do to look after ourselves.

Be aware of the different kinds of bullying, understand them and deal with them if they happen to you or those around you.

Consequences of being bullied include anxiety, a fear of going to school, feelings of being both unsafe and unhappy at school, and low self-esteem[81].

CYBER-BULLYING

In the past, coming home meant you could at least be safe until the next school day. But in today's world, bullies can also get you on Facebook and other channels, meaning there's often nowhere to hide.

Students can torment each other online and can do so from the safety of being behind a computer or phone screen. Cyber-bullying is a growing threat and with technology advancing at such speed, the potential for online bullying to flourish is a major concern.

"Because everyone is so connected now – and connected all the time – it's just endless, whereas before you dealt with bullies at school and then that was it, you didn't see them after school," Tony said. "You cannot escape it, and teenagers particularly tend to live by texts, live on their phones and social media sites."

> Cyber-bullying is a significant issue for young people, overlapping with existing face-to-face bullying attacks[82]. In California, almost one quarter of all teenagers report having been threatened online by a peer or classmate.

This new form of bullying can cause higher levels of depression and anxiety than more traditional forms of bullying, and has been linked to incidents of youth suicide.

"What girls look at is how many people have liked that mean comment [said about them by a bully] ... if one person has said something mean, and then 100 people have liked that comment, it is even more damaging [to the victim]," Lisa Farrow explained.

This "piling on" has the effect of reinforcing the abuse, she says, which serves to affirm the bully's message in the victim's eyes, compared to a scenario in which no one, or only a handful of people, affirmed the message.

> Female high school students are the second most likely group to be cyber-bullied, with one in five teenage girls saying that they have experienced some form of online abuse or harassment[83].

The only group more likely to suffer from such abuse is LGBTQI students[84].

Students may also feel bullied by virtue of not being included in certain activities, and then having their faces rubbed in it online.

"There were instances, when I was young, where I saw an event on Facebook or saw all of my friends together, and I realised that I hadn't been invited or hadn't been included," Sophia said.

"It's a different kind of bullying and rejection, because it's not necessarily direct discrimination, it's indirect … sometimes, that hurts much more."

So what can you do?

One benefit of social media is the option to pick and choose who you connect with. Ensuring you are only connected with those whom you want to engage with, and who won't hurt you, is crucial.

"Eventually what [my daughter] did – and it took her a while to come around to the idea – was 'un-friending' all those people [bullying her], so she wasn't seeing the messages all the time," Tony said.

"Facebook can be a weapon of choice, so clear your account and get rid of all of those kids [who bully], so you have a very small group who you are communicating with."

You can also just stop all social media. But it's not necessarily realistic, nor is it fair when you haven't done anything wrong.

Instead, try to find a middle ground whereby you can enjoy the good that comes with social media while also protecting yourself from the bad.

But you may not always be able to steer clear of online bullies, even if you can better curate your audience. Fellow students, or even older people, who wish to harm you and others sometimes set up fake accounts or profiles.

Document any and all harmful communication.

Fifty-four per cent of young people identifying as lesbian, gay or transgender report being cyber-bullied[85].

Unlike face-to-face bullying, where it is more difficult to prove that it's actually occurred, screen shots or printouts of teasing and insults can help you prevent it from happening in the future. If it's happening to you tell someone about it immediately.

PLAYGROUND, CLASSROOM BULLYING

Teenagers who are bullied can suffer bed-wetting, trouble sleeping, anxiety, depression, school phobia, insecurity, unhappiness, loneliness, isolation, and somatic symptoms[86].

My mates from high school are great guys. But it's fair to say that a couple of them were bullies. In Year 10 one of the guys (let's call him Ron) was dating a girl from a school up the road. A rumour started that another guy (we'll call him Gary) had been hitting on Ron's girlfriend.

Ron was already not a huge fan of Gary and he used this as an excuse to attack him – with the help of some willing participants. The drama eventually became physical, but Ron got the better of Gary, because he had help from others. It ended with him pouring a tin of tuna on Gary's school shirt, which he had to wear back to class after lunch.

Gary was always a confident, charming kid – and he still is. But this day at school really rocked him … after a few tears and a desperate scrub of his shirt at the bubblers, he headed back to class and put on a brave face.

I'm pretty sure the teachers never found out. The rest of us certainly didn't say anything. That was just within our own friendship group.

There were also times when other guys in our year copped it; being pushed into lockers or playground bins, being verbally taunted for (supposedly) being gay, or being pelted with food just because it was funny to the rest of us.

We had our 10-year class reunion in 2015. At that gathering, a few of my mates approached those who had been victims of the occasional taunt. Some of them were able to laugh off the childhood incidents and have a good chat. Others, however, told my mates to get lost. They remembered being bullied, and wanted nothing to do with any classmate who had upset them.

Bullying might seem funny to those with the power. I know I found it funny sometimes to see others get mocked. But, for the victims, it is a different story.

> Forty per cent of Indigenous young people are worried about bullying, compared to 33.9% of non-Indigenous young people[87].

Face-to-face bullying is still a major source of distress for many high school students. And, as Katie Bennett noted, it can distort your world view.

"When you're being bullied, it's hard to see that life's ever going to be different. That's your window into what your future is going to look like," she said.

Passive, interpersonal bullying is just as bad.

"Girls like to exclude, rather than [engage in] overt bullying, by starting rumours and saying, 'Don't talk to her, we don't like her today' – subtly excluding someone from the group," Lisa Farrow said.

As social creatures, we need to be accepted and included in a tribe. When that's threatened it can be devastating, especially to a young person, who may then feel as though their world is falling apart.

"Covert bullying such as this can make a school student endlessly question not only what it is they did wrong, but also their self-worth," said Eileen Condell, a Sydney-based psychotherapist and counsellor for young people. Being isolated socially "can cause anxiety, depression, and feelings of worthlessness – some of the things that can lead a young person to possibly contemplate suicide," she added.

No high school student should be bullied. But while it is important for you to respond and not ignore it, don't inflame the situation by responding in kind.

"Rather than going on the attack, which unfortunately our daughter did, it would have been better for her to try not to address it directly with them, and to speak to her teachers, because they are the people who are going to support her, not the ones who were attacking her," Tony said. "Escalating things herself just made things worse. Bullies bully somebody, and it's pretty hard when they keep at you. But if you can avoid showing that it's affecting you they tend to lose interest."

Talk to the right people. Your parents are the first port of call. Teachers, guidance counsellors at school and other support staff will not only be able to take meaningful action, but do so in a way that is sensitive to how you feel.

"[Our daughter] had a couple of teachers, and other support networks at the school, through counsellors and the chaplains, who were able to help her through and protect her as much as they possibly could, and teaching her how to cope," Tony said.

We don't always have the right answers – especially when it comes to being attacked by our classmates and supposed friends, either on social media or at school. But there are steps you can take to stop it.

I know it's scary ... taking action might even seem like an escalation of the situation. But seeking immediate help is the best way for you to not only put a stop to bullying but also ensure your own health and wellbeing.

TWD WELLBEING WISDOM

While your experience of bullying will be unique, the steps you can take to look after yourself are the same for everyone. If you are the victim of bullying in any form, no matter how trivial, try the following:

- **Seek immediate help**. Telling your parents or teachers doesn't make you weak, or a snitch. Self-protection is important and you have a duty to look after yourself and your own wellbeing.

- **Don't respond in kind**. Most bullies are looking for a reaction, such as a sign that you are upset, which they may take as justification for their abuse. Not responding will likely cause the bully to move on.

- **Curate your online connections**. Only connect and engage with people who bring value and pleasure to your use of social media. Social media should be a space where you can relax, have fun and enjoy meaningful relationships.

- **Don't share too much of yourself**. It's easy to post your innermost thoughts and feelings, but be careful about who you're sharing your information with, as it can provide ammunition to others who may wish to harm you.

- **Keep evidence of the incident**. If you are able to go to a teacher or parent with proof that another student has bullied you, it is highly unlikely that abuse will occur again.

- **Discuss how you feel with people you trust**. Even after you have taken steps to stop the bullying, talk about it with your parents, friends, teachers … whomever you feel comfortable with.

Let's talk about sex, baby

"I had boyfriends in high school and I was labelled a slut. But either you're a slut or a freak [for not having boyfriends] ... you can't really win either way."

Sex – whether you're having it or not – is a natural part of life. And sexuality isn't just about sex. It's also about body image, intimacy, attraction and affection, and the development and maintenance of relationships.

Sexuality is influenced by your thoughts, feelings and desires, your past experiences, your friends and community, even your culture, background, religion, media and popular culture[88].

As a form of exercise, sex can help lower your blood pressure and lead to a healthier heart rate[89]. It can decrease stress, and can help us feel more relaxed, in the same way as meditation might[90]. Sex can boost our immune systems[91] and make us feel healthier (especially if we are in love)[92]. Even just hugging can lower blood pressure and help relieve stress and tension[93].

Without doubt, sex has the potential to make us healthier and happier!

But the research proves that casual sex – especially when you're in your teens – can have a negative impact on your health and wellbeing.

Many teenagers who have sex while at school will not suffer anxiety or depression, but those who have sex earlier than their peers, and whose relationships are uncommitted and ultimately fall apart, are at a much greater risk[94].

Those issues differ depending on your circumstances, but being in a relationship that ends, particularly if it ends badly, can cause social problems and therefore mental health problems, on top of whatever sexual stuff you are working through.

"She [our daughter] had a relationship with a guy who was

one of the prefects of the school and one of the more popular kids. When the relationship broke down, she was pretty well ostracised, and her tight friendship group basically ran out," Tony said.

Lisa Farrow agreed, noting the ways teens explore their sexuality can also come back to haunt them. "[The boys will] request that one of our girls send him a photo of her wearing very little, and because she's very fond of that person, she'll do so," she said. "But then they might break up, and within a very short time frame, that photo is circulated to his mates, and all of a sudden it's all around that boy's school."

Similar to relationship breakdown issues, teens who have casual sex (as opposed to sex in a relationship) are more likely to suffer from depression than their peers[95].

And it goes the other way. Teenagers who are depressed, or show signs of depression or even suicidal tendencies, are more likely to engage in casual sex both while at school and then as young adults; this then can lead to further deterioration in your health in later life[96].

Having sex, or engaging in sexual activities, at too early an age can hurt your academic performance – especially for girls[97]. School marks suffer more for girls than for boys if sex occurs early, because girls are often thought to be more relationship-oriented[98]. In addition, the physical risks of sex – such as pregnancy and STIs –

can lead to greater psychological and social effects with girls[99].

Sophia noticed this among her female peers at school.

"A lot of young girls feel like their sexuality is their currency in high school, and that being sexual beings at such a young age makes them cool. I would say if you're not ready and prepared then you need to wait, because you need to be comfortable and assured in yourself before you allow other people to be engaging with you," Sophia said.

But no matter what some people do, there will be those who will want to put labels on you.

"I had boyfriends in high school and I was labelled a slut. But either you're a slut or a freak [for not having boyfriends] … you can't really win either way," Flynne said.

Peer pressure is enormous when it comes to sex, especially in this day and age in which we are saturated with sexually-charged material on social media, in popular culture, and in our everyday conversations and activities.

Another issue – regardless of how sexually active you are – is being able accept who you are, and what your sexual orientation is.

For Sam C., acceptance of his homosexuality as a high school student was a turning point for his mental health and wellbeing. It was, however, a monumental challenge for him to navigate.

"I saw the victimisation of other gay people in my life, and I spent too many years trying to escape the reality of my identity," he said.

This need to escape isn't confined to LGBTQI students – others notice it, too.

"There was a stigma about coming out as gay. There was

definitely a need to label people, like someone was straight or gay, and that's what they were," Flynne said.

"I know a few people who really struggled throughout high school because they felt they had to hide their homosexuality or bisexuality, and that makes me really sad because I feel like everyone should be able to be comfortable and assured in their own skin," Sophia said.

Finding someone to date is never easy! This is especially true for LGBTQI students, whose pool of potential partners is smaller.

"Dating can be particularly hard for young people, because the population of potential partners is nowhere near that of our heterosexual peers," Sam C. explained.

Whether you are straight or gay, a boyfriend or girlfriend can offer security, companionship, intimacy, trust and fun. If your potential dating pool is smaller, it makes it a lot harder to find fun and romance, and this can reinforce feelings of isolation.

"High school should provide an opportunity to try new things and make mistakes – especially in developing relationships – such as learning how to interact with each other emotionally, learning about changes to your body and emotions, and so on. But if it's somehow taboo, or not talked about openly, then it makes things a lot harder," Luke Furness said.

Sex is a pleasurable activity. It can be a kind of self-medication, or diversion, or even a kind of attention-seeking behaviour[100].

I'm not going to tell you that you shouldn't have sex. Aside from the fact that abstinence policies don't work, you are starting to grow and develop, and you should have both the freedom and luxury to explore life how you see fit, to the extent that you are safe and not hurting yourself or anyone else.

And it's not as though anything I say will likely stop you: roughly a quarter of Year 10 students and half of Year 12 students have had sex, and almost 40% of Year 10 students and almost 60% of Year 12 students have had oral sex[101].

You must strike the right balance. Be aware, be safe, and be smart.

Just make sure that any sexual experiences you have are done right, and with the right person. Having sex or engaging in sexual activities in the 'wrong' way will have detrimental effects on your health and wellbeing.

TWD WELLBEING WISDOM

Sex is everywhere and an awareness of the issues, how they can affect us, and how we can look after ourselves, is the best way that we can ensure our own health and wellbeing.

Here are a few things that I wish I'd be more aware of when I was your age.

- **Sex isn't just about getting off**[102]. Unlike animals, humans have sex for more than just biological reproductive purposes. We have sex for pleasure, passion, boredom, anger, happiness, sadness ... the works! And because sex is therefore part of our personal, social and emotional lives, we have to talk openly about it. Only by talking about can we deal with issues like shame, privacy, responsibility, awkwardness, and so on.

- **Always respect personal boundaries – yours and others'**. Just because you're up for anything doesn't mean the other person is. Make sure you understand what your partner wants or doesn't want, whether it's discussing fantasies or consent. Communicate openly about how you feel, what you want and what you value.

- **Whether you're having sex or not doesn't say anything about your worth as a person**. High school can be a brutal place – both boys and girls get teased for either not having sex, or having too much. As Flynne said, you can't win either way.

But allowing your personal value to be determined by your sexual activity is a slippery slope. Stand your ground and don't do anything you're not comfortable with.

- **Your sexual orientation is completely natural**. Two points to make here: one, if you're curious about your sexuality and want to explore your thoughts and feelings, don't feel ashamed. Don't repress it. It's crucial that you figure out who you are and what you want. Two, being in a sexual "minority", such as gay or lesbian, doesn't mean you're in any way abnormal. It doesn't even mean you're different. It's just who you are.

- **Have fun!** If you are having sex, or "doing other stuff", having fun should be front of your mind (alongside being safe). If it's not an enjoyable experience for you, then don't do it. Put your wellbeing, and that of your partner, first. And don't feel guilty.

- **No sex? No worries!** Feeling like a loser because some of your mates are having sex, but you're not? Guess what … you're not the first, and you certainly won't be the last. Don't agonise and let it stress you out … your time will come. You're no less awesome than anyone else.

Getting into the substances: alcohol, smoking, and drug taking

"Where my friends would drink to dance and have a good time, I would drink to tranquillise my feelings. I would wake up every morning conscious of the void that I was convinced was only satiable with vodka or scotch."

It shouldn't come as a surprise to learn that teenagers who don't drink alcohol have higher self-esteem than those who do[103], as well as being less confident[104]. Those who drink often suffer from dislike of self, social withdrawal, pessimism, have a sense of failure, complain about their body and be preoccupied with bodily function[105].

"It's not just an outlet – it's about trying to do something that allows you to forget your problems," Tony said. "There are a number of kids [at my son's school] that we know aren't coping who have used drugs. And because they're all getting older, they also have access to alcohol, and many kids don't tend to handle that too well."

Milly described how drinking on the weekends was an escape. It gave you something to look forward to and allowed you to take your mind off everything that was going on.

"You could go to an 18th [birthday] or house party, and get really, really pissed, as it was a time for us to relax. You have such a busy, active work schedule and you just want to party with your friends and not think about school," she said.

It wasn't necessarily a good thing, Milly conceded, despite making her feel better at the time.

For Sam C., the need to escape went beyond a simple desire to let loose with friends … it was a necessary crutch in order to get through the week.

"Where my friends would drink to dance and have a good time, I would drink to tranquillise my feelings. I would wake up every morning conscious of the void that I was convinced was only satiable with vodka or scotch," he said.

You don't need me to tell you how dangerous this is – not just because of the impact it can have on your mental wellbeing, but also your physical health.

Even if you are not dabbling with substances of any kind,

you may find that your wellbeing suffers because it can be hard to say no to your friends.

"I stayed away from social occasions where there was a lot of smoking, taking drugs and drinking … but it's really hard to do that when you're young and you want to impress," Sophia said. "It wasn't a lot of fun because I ended up turning down a lot of invitations because I didn't drink, and I didn't feel the need to be there."

Shutting yourself off from fun activities is, ironically, not great for your wellbeing either. It's important to unwind and relax with friends. So what can you do?

"Surround yourself with people who you really trust, that you can rely on, and who love you for who you are, and can be yourself around, and not just be friends with them because it looks cool," Alicia said. "I think that's a really important part of Year 12."

Ensuring you're around such people, in turn, makes it easier for you to make smart choices.

"What's more impressive than trying things before you're ready is actually being sure about yourself and the choices that you're making. If you're not ready or prepared [for alcohol, smoking or drug taking], then you need to be honest about that and you need to stay true to your beliefs and values," Sophia said.

There is also an important role for parents to play.

"If alcohol and drugs are a normal part of our daily and social lives [as parents], it will be indelibly etched into our children's ideals about what activities are involved with socialising," said Maria Bulgar, a Brisbane-based parent. "I don't think we should hide alcohol consumption from children if it is part of our lives. That would be hypocritical. However, it is about demonstrating moderation. We need to show them, as they learn mostly by observing us, that we can enjoy ourselves socially *without* alcohol. And if we are drinking, we don't have to drink to excess. We also need to show them that we don't turn to alcohol to help us cope with stress. We also need to make drugs and alcohol part of an ongoing conversation, not just the big talk once every so often."

Choosing to have a drink, or smoke, or take pills can be a really tough choice to make when it's in front of you. You might be naturally curious, or feel the need to conform or impress your mates, even though you know it's dangerous.

There are a number of things to bear in mind when in these sorts of situation, whether you are an active participant or not. See the next page for advice.

TWD WELLBEING WISDOM

When it comes to looking after your health and wellbeing, engage in activities that are healthy and fun, help you relax, and achieve a balance. Always remember to be safe. If you're trying to change your habits, give the following a go:

- **Get your friends' support**. Let them know if you're trying to cut down, and have them hold you to that promise.
- **Leave parties early**. If the heavy drinking or smoking happens later at night, leave earlier to ensure that you're not tempted.
- **Do other things to distract yourself**. Keep up other activities that allow you to escape and have fun. Go dancing, listen to music, play games and sports, have a Netflix binge … whatever you want.
- **Employ specific wellbeing strategies**. Do regular exercise, and practise meditation or mindfulness to tackle stress and anxiety.
- **Talk to someone**. If you feel like drinking, drugs or smoking are affecting you, making you more stressed and anxious, ask a doctor, counsellor or other health professional for support.
- **Don't be too strict on yourself**. You don't have to be a saint to be healthy and happy … you're

allowed the occasional indulgence. But always remember that drugs, alcohol and smoking are ultimately detrimental to your physical and emotional wellbeing, and there are better ways to relieve the pressure.

Realistically, I know that many of you reading this will still occasionally drink, smoke or dabble in drugs. It's inevitable that we will experiment and want to learn more about ourselves and the world. But there's no escaping the fact that such substances are dangerous (and illegal), especially when you're young.

Here are some suggestions for dealing with alcohol, cigarettes or drugs:

- **Set limits**. If you must indulge, try to minimise your intake by setting a number – for example, two drinks or one cigarette – and get a friend to hold you to those self-imposed limits.

- **Don't do it alone**: Make sure you're in the company of family or friends if you drink, smoke or take drugs. You have no way of predicting how your body will react, so take precautions.

- **Be conscious of what you're doing.** I mean this in two ways. One, don't indulge to the point that you are no longer conscious of what is going on. And two, remember that you're choosing to escape with drugs or alcohol, and know that there are plenty of healthier ways to manage your wellbeing.

Is Year 12 and my ATAR the be all and end all?

"There's this idea that Year 12 is the be all and end all, and if you don't do well, then you're going to mess up the rest of your life. It's a complete fallacy ... there are always options."

Your marks at school are important. But they don't determine the course of your life. Need proof? Former British Prime Minister, Sir Winston Churchill, was – as a teenager – described as follows:

"Winston possessed no discernible talent for hard work. The boy seemed to drift through life doing the absolute bare minimum to get by, all the while maintaining a very high opinion of himself. As far as [his parents] could tell, his son was sorely lacking in common sense and intelligence[106]*."*

He may have drifted through high school, but Churchill went on to become one of Britain's most distinguished and famous leaders. Supposedly neither talented nor intelligent, he helped defeat Hitler!

There are a few lessons here: one, you can do anything you want. Two, retain your sense of self-worth and confidence. And three, high school is not the only avenue to success.

If you fall into the trap of believing that your value is dictated by your numerical grades, your wellness will suffer.

The ATAR is a good indicator of how well you performed in particular subjects and exams, and no more. It's not a marker of your worth as a working professional in the future, or as a person. But this doesn't stop many high school students from feeling like the ATAR represents their personal value.

"I was certainly under the impression that my ATAR was the be all and end all. I lived and breathed for it – I would spend so long on the online ATAR predictor websites, seeing what marks I had to get in order to achieve the ATAR I wanted (and I would only have been happy with 99)," Chelsea said. "I think getting good marks was used as the only measure of intelligence, potential and work ethic, and I honestly believed that my entire 13 years of schooling came down to that one number … that's how important it was made out to be."

Pressure to achieve a good ATAR can come from the school itself: sometimes, student performance is used as a marketing tool. In the case of private schools, saying that a large number of your Year 12 students achieved top marks can be a way to justify higher fees. For public or state schools, showcasing academic achievement is useful in seeking government funding.

As a result, students often feel the heat from their teachers or principal to get certain grades for the good of the school. But this isn't fair, and does nothing to alleviate your anxiety about marks.

"One of my teachers told us that, 'The higher your ATAR, the more doors will be open for you at university'. She meant well – and technically she was right – but to us it meant, 'If you do badly, you will not have many options to get into a good degree and, therefore, get a high-paying job or even one you enjoy'. Obviously, this scared us, so we increased the pressure to do better than our best," Holly M. said.

How do you respond? Especially if it feels like your world is dictated by your achievements at school alone?

During the penultimate year of my law and communications degree, I got a summer clerkship with one of the big commercial law firms in Sydney. These positions were highly sought after and I thought – as did many of my friends and classmates – that getting a position in a big firm would set us up for our legal careers. I had my heart set on it.

Halfway through my clerkship, however, I had my breakdown at the Falls Festival. When I realised the extent of my health problems I was overwhelmed to the point that I felt like I couldn't properly function. I stumbled and struggled through the remainder of the clerkship, knowing that I wasn't performing at a level I knew I was capable of. Nevertheless, I was convinced that I would ultimately be offered a graduate job by the firm. In the end I was the only summer clerk not kept on as a grad.

It was devastating. I had worked so hard and placed so much emphasis on achieving this. I felt as though I had failed, and that I would get left behind in my career struggling to survive, whereas all of my law buddies would go on to make millions. Throw in the fact that I had just been diagnosed with clinical depression and anxiety, I was a mess. Figuring out how to recover from this professional gut punch was beyond me.

But like getting a low ATAR, not being offered a graduate job simply meant that I had to forge a different path. It actually gave me more freedom to dictate how that path unfolded. If it weren't for that failure, I wouldn't have had the opportunity to work for the Royal Commission into Institutional Responses to Child Sexual Abuse (a role as meaningful as it was intense). I wouldn't have been able to do the legal academic and research work I did. I wouldn't have had the idea to write my first book, *The Wellness Doctrines for Law Students and Young Lawyers*, which means I wouldn't have given lectures internationally, become a renowned consultant for law firms and universities, or a life coach to law students.

And of course I wouldn't have written the book you are now reading.

"I told my boys that it didn't necessarily matter what their final results were, because there are so many pathways now," Rachael said.

Not being offered a graduate lawyer position at a big law firm was just that; it was not an indictment on my career, or on my life. The same is true for you while at high school. Pree Benton explained that there are many success stories of people who failed at school but have gone on to enjoy successful careers.

"One of my girlfriends at school scored 40 points lower than what she was expecting, and she felt like her life was over," she said. "But she found a way through with alternative study, which got her into university. Now she's a highly successful manager for an international finance organisation and is thriving in her career."

Katie Bennett told me a similar story about her husband. "He didn't do well in school, and now he's an incredibly successful manager for an international finance company. What is detrimental is the idea that [final exams] are going to represent your potential and opportunity for success in the future," she said.

"There are so many things that contribute to your success and career path, such as your courage, capabilities, willingness to put yourself out there, your creativity and your personality."

If you do not do well in Year 12, or as well as you would have wanted, you may not immediately be able to do what you want to do. It is not true, however, that failing to achieve your goals at high school means you have failed or that you are a failure.

Your ATAR is *not* a life sentence.

"Chances are, things will happen in life that you won't expect, and will open doors to other paths you hadn't thought of. Have a plan, but remember that you can switch and change," said Peter.

If you don't get the marks to get into a particular uni degree, you might have to start another degree, or consider TAFE, and then transfer later on. Or you could wait to study your chosen degree as a postgraduate after doing another course. You can also decide to forgo further study altogether and find a job instead. You might discover a real flair for business, which helps you to earn real money.

In this day and age, the options are endless. Gone are the days where the die is cast and the number of job opportunities can be counted on one hand. There are a million ways to get to where you want to be, or discover what you want to do.

The ATAR is a good indicator of how well you perform in particular subjects and exams, and no more. It is not a marker of your worth as a working professional in the future, or as an individual.

> "The number you get at the end of Year 12 does not decide your life, no matter what anyone says," Mitch Wallis said.

Katie Bennett felt empowered and supported by those teachers who championed acceptance and encouragement more than competition.

"They didn't put too much pressure on the mark, but rather on who I was and my potential. They gave me the courage and encouragement to do my best, and told me it didn't matter what I got in the end as long as I gave it my all," she said.

In the grand scheme of things, your marks in Year 12 are just a blip on the radar.

While some of you might think you'll need to tattoo your ATAR to your forehead when leaving school in order to get ahead, the truth is that – aside from initial entries into tertiary study – your marks at school will almost never be brought up in a job interview or any other context. Frankly ... no one in the outside world cares!

What matters more is who you are as a person.

Try not to stress about Year 12 and your ATAR. Yes, it's an important year; one of the most important of your life to date. But there's much more in store beyond what happens when you are 16 and 17. These years are not the be all and end all. They're just the beginning of your journey.

TWD WELLBEING WISDOM

- **Only you can define your worth and path in life.** Nobody knows you better than the person who looks back at you in the mirror. Take time to understand and appreciate who you are, and who you want to be. Don't worry about what other people are doing … what you make of yourself post-school is up to you.

- **Your marks are a reflection of performance in senior school – no more.** You might not become Prime Minister, but there is no reason why you can't succeed once you walk out of those school gates for the last time, even if you haven't done as well as you wanted to.

- **No matter the outcome … there is life after Year 12.** If you're not happy with your final performance, remember that there are a million ways to get to where you want to be. Take a bridging course to get into the degree you want, or transfer from another degree. Find a job that will give you transferable skills. Explore the world and discover new opportunities. It's your oyster, after all.

- **Seek advice from as many people as you can.** If you're struggling to find perspective, talk to those who have "been there, done that". They'll tell you that life goes on, that your marks in high school don't matter in the real world, and they'll advise on how best you can get through those stressful times.

- **Hold your head up high and look to the future.** The end of high school is only the beginning. While your final exams may seem like the end of the world, they're not. You have so much more life to live, and – from now on – you have much more freedom and autonomy in choosing how that life unfolds.

What should I do when I leave school?

The short answer is … whatever you want!

"It's really, really okay to not know where you want to be for the rest of your life at 16–17 years old," Mitch Wallis said.

Despite doing pretty well in Years 11 and 12, enjoying my time at school and knowing that I wanted to study communications, I also knew that I needed a break. The idea of taking a gap year, getting away from study and thoughts about the future, was top of mind for me.

I applied for and got a placement with a volunteer company, Lattitude Global Volunteering, to do a six-month stint in Vanuatu. Along with some British and other Australian students I taught schoolkids in the remote islands. I was paired with an English guy and stationed on an island of 30 square kilometres; we shared a bamboo hut overlooking the ocean, walked up to the high school every morning to teach classes, and then swimming in the afternoon.

There was no running water or electricity and I could only communicate with my parents via a village-wide telephone about once a week. And while that was a scary prospect at first for a kid who had been sheltered his whole life – it was ultimately character-building and life-affirming.

> A gap year was the best thing I could possibly have done. I was able to get the physical and emotional distance I needed from the rigours of Years 11 and 12, get out my comfort zone, grow into adulthood and experience life in a completely foreign environment.

While overseas, I was struck by the extraordinary relationship between poverty and happiness. Despite surviving hand to mouth in rusty shacks, with TV viewable only via a community generator, and no Internet access or mobile phones, the villagers couldn't have been happier. They seemed unaware of the burdens of the developed world and were able to live a simple lifestyle that provided all that they truly needed. It was eye opening to say the least.

While I haven't been able to retain all those island life practices I promised to bring back with me – I gave up on cold bucket showers almost immediately in favour of hot running water, for example – it was, and remains, an important period of my life and one for which I am eternally grateful.

Of course, a gap year is not for everyone. Deciding what to do when you finish school can be stressful. It can seem like the biggest decision of your life, and it may well be. Ultimately, it doesn't matter what road you take, so long as it is your decision.

> Katie Bennett said the first step is figuring out exactly what this would look like for you: "Understand that the right path isn't what society defines as the right path. It's about what it means for you."

Getting advice from other people (like me!) is important in making as informed a decision as possible. But having the strength to choose your own path is the only way you can ensure you are doing something that will make you healthy and happy.

Here are some options for you to consider when you leave school:

GO TO UNIVERSITY OR TAFE

For many of you, getting into university is the ultimate achievement of high school. It is, literally, what the ATAR is set up for. And you may impatient to get started and get on your way to becoming an adult.

Studying at university or TAFE offers an educational experience unlike anything you will have experienced before. It is also much more catered to an adult lifestyle … no uniforms, classes at times of your choosing, and the flexibility to work part-time simultaneously. Starting tertiary study right away can feel like you're making real strides towards earning the big bucks.

> "I encouraged my son to pick something that he was interested in. I said to him that he was going to have to get out of bed to go to lectures, and he had to be interested enough to do that. If he wasn't interested, he should pick something else," Rachael said.

But first and second year tertiary students can also find themselves burnt out after high school. They haven't had enough time to recuperate from those stressful senior years. They end up taking a semester or two off, or even changing degrees. There's nothing wrong with this … but trust me when I say that burning out is not much fun. If you're to go straight to uni, be mindful of the dangers of burnout and take added precautions.

You should also consider whether continuing to study is something that you truly want to do.

"I think there's huge pressure on people to go to uni nowadays," Pree Benton said. "There's a kind of societal belief – which seems to have increased over the last couple of decades – that you're not successful unless you've done some sort of tertiary education."

This is absolutely not the case.

Some of the most successful people in the world never went to or finished uni – Mark Zuckerberg, the founder and CEO of Facebook, being the most prominent example.

It is important for you to remember that in this day and age there are more avenues for success without tertiary qualifications than ever before.

Camellia is an advocate of doing tertiary study, especially if you do not yet know what you want to do with your life. Tertiary study can help you make a more informed decision.

"I tell [my students who do not know what they want] to do an arts degree first up, because it gives you a taste test. You can do English subjects, law subjects, philosophy, language, maths … you can do pretty much whatever you want. This is the most productive year you can have in early adulthood – that was my experience … I figured out what I wanted to do with the rest of my life in that year," she said.

"Students need to treat university not as a key that opens the door to the rest of your life, but as a stage to go through in order to figure out which door they're going to choose to open. The key is always going to be there for them in the end … it's just a matter of choosing which path you're going to go down."

Sam C. agreed with this. "It's a far better option to go and start uni, finish first year, and then re-assess. If you really want to travel, finish your degree, get that piece of paper and use it as your ticket to work abroad for a while."

If you feel like you need to go to university, but aren't quite sure of your direction, give Sam and Camellia's approach a go. You will lose nothing, and only stand to gain experience and insight.

FIND A JOB

Going straight into a full-time job (for example, police, defence forces), or an apprenticeship (for example, plumbing, carpentry, hairdressing), can lead you towards the career you want. You may even be lucky enough to find a job in a small business that requires no further study. This can be a great way to bide your time productively, developing your professional skills while putting some money in the bank.

No matter the job, it's important to learn and grow from the role. Working in a bar, for example, can make for a great pathway towards hospitality management. If you don't have a proper plan for your job, it is easy to become disenchanted and lost.

"Go and learn in an environment you're comfortable in. If you dream of an apprenticeship, or something in an industry that you could derive a lot of enjoyment from, pursue it. Just remember, whatever you do, don't stop learning," Sam C. said.

TAKE A GAP YEAR

I found taking a gap year a necessity after the stress of Years 11 and 12. I needed to get out, have a break, lie on the beach for a while, meet new people and clear my head.

By the time I returned home, I was itching to resume studying and was ready to tackle my double degree. I couldn't have gone straight to university with such motivation had I not taken that year off to travel.

Flynne agreed even though she did the opposite.

"I regret not taking a gap year, because now that I'm in my course [at university], I feel as though I would have been better equipped for it if I'd had a year to myself. I went from a year of working really hard to another year of working really hard, and another ... I'm still doing that," she said.

> You might worry that, if you take a year off to go travelling, you won't be able to get back into study. But I have not met one person who has ever come back from a gap year and not still wanted to pursue their chosen course.

"Parents become very concerned when you stray from the path that you've been on. The risk is that you won't be able to get back into study … but more often than not, the opposite is true," Flynne said.

You may also fear that you'll fall behind your peers … this, too, is false. Life is not a race whereby you have to be married by 25 and have kids by 30! Doing things at your own pace and not comparing yourself to others helps avoid competitiveness which, as we saw in another chapter, can cause anxiety.

> What a gap year can provide for you – aside from a chance to be free and become your own person – is an opportunity to reflect on what it is you really want.

"Gap years are a great time for young people to develop the savviness, independence, clarity and emotional skills needed to make better decisions for themselves, rather than just thinking of what would please others," Dr Jenny Brockis said.

A gap year doesn't mean your career has stalled. It's a chance for you to make a more informed decision about what you want do to and what kind of person you want to be. This is what Chris Gould found, when visiting his son in Thailand.

"He's become enormously independent, very frugal, and it's given him the chance to grow as a person away from the family and pursue his own spirituality," he said. "He'll be coming back as a more confident, independent person, who will be more prepared for university compared to someone coming straight out of Year 12."

"Not knowing what you want is normal. All pathways that you will take when you walk out of the school gates are going to have benefits to them," Amba Brown, a positive psychology author, said.

Ultimately, it comes down to three things: one, whatever you do post-school is your decision; two, it's okay not to have a clue about what comes next; and three, whatever path you choose, there will be personal and vocational benefits – so long as you utilise them properly.

TWD WELLBEING WISDOM

> "Just keep moving forward, because eventually you will figure out what you like and don't like, and you can steer your life from there," said Amba Brown.

Deciding on a path – or the first step of your path – is not easy. Here are a few quick tips to help you make the most informed choices.

- **Do what you want, not what you think you should do**. You may feel pressured to study a certain degree, or take up a particular job because your parents or teachers say it will be best for you. But nobody knows you better than yourself. Trust yourself.

- **That said, seek advice from others**. Those who have "been there, done that" will be able to offer advice and relate experiences which will help. Soak up as much as you can and try to picture yourself in the different scenarios so you work out what fits best.

- **Nothing is irrevocable**. The road you choose right after school won't set the tone for the rest of your life. You can always change direction. Don't like your degree? Transfer. Had enough of your job? Go travelling, or enrol in tertiary study. You're young … nothing is set in stone yet.

- **Not having a clue is not a problem.** If you're an 18 year old who knows exactly what you want, I am hugely impressed. Many 40–50 year olds haven't a clue what they want! Don't put pressure on yourself to figure out your whole life now … just do what makes you happy and things will flow from there.

- **Don't discount any options that even remotely spark your interest**[107]. Keep an open mind about different avenues you can take before narrowing them down to a shortlist of ideas.

SOLUTIONS

Where there are problems, there are always solutions! Listed in this next section is a range of strategies you could employ to better manage your health and wellbeing. Not every idea will be for you ... but reading about what others have been through, and what has worked for them, will give you inspiration. Remember … be proactive, not reactive. Get ahead of the game, look after yourself before issues arise, and be the healthiest and happiest high school student you can possibly be.

What *doesn't* work?

Happily, despite the inevitable issues you're going to have to navigate in high school to stay healthy and happy, there are heaps of ways that you can look after yourself so you're well prepared.

A word of warning, though: some strategies might actually make you feel worse, prolong a problem, or cause longer-term consequences, so be careful! What often appears to be a solution in the short term can often turn out to be detrimental in the long term. Here are just a few things you *should not* do.

DOING NOTHING

Mental health issues should be treated in the same way as any other illness. If you have a headache, you take a tablet to feel better. If you break your leg, you have a doctor put a cast on so it can heal.

The same logic applies if you feel stressed. Do something to relieve the pressure!

"If you sprained your ankle in the playground, you wouldn't just walk around for the rest of the day limping ... you'd go and get it looked at, you'd put a bandage on it and make sure you were going to be okay," Sophia said. "Treat your mental health just as you would look your physical health. If you don't address that sprained ankle, you're going to be walking with a limp for a long time. It's exactly the same with your mental wellbeing ... if you don't address it, and get the help that you need, you're going to suffer in the years to come."

> Doing nothing – no matter how trivial your stress or anxiety may seem – is not the answer. "For a while, I tried to ignore my mental illness because I thought it would go away on its own," Sam C. said. "I couldn't understand why every other kid could cope with school except me."

I'm probably the last person who should be telling you that by doing nothing you are making things worse. I didn't take any action about my own mental health issues until I'd already suffered a major breakdown. If I didn't take action why should you?

I hope my experience will serve as a cautionary tale. I desperately wish that I had done more to manage my health and wellbeing before it became a serious problem. I might have been able to avoid my breakdown and depression altogether.

I say this not to scare you; but if you're feeling stressed, anxious or blue, there is always something you can do, or someone you can talk to. Take advantage of the resources available.

Doing something is *always* better than doing nothing.

There is not a single thing to be lost by looking into ways to be healthier and happier – but failing to take that step can absolutely make things worse. Don't do what I did. Get ahead of an issue before it becomes worse!

ENERGY DRINKS

The manufacturers of drinks like Red Bull and V say their products will boost your concentration levels but overwhelmingly research shows that these beverages do more harm than good.

Teenagers who are already prone to psychological distress, anxiety and

> depression are more likely to consume energy drinks, making those health concerns worse[108].

I can understand the appeal of energy drinks. They're cheap, tasty and they give you a massive sugar high. But in reality the downsides outweigh the supposed benefits.

Whenever I drink them, I can't fall asleep properly because my heart's pounding. The sugar makes me feel queasy. Gaining an extra 30 minutes or so doesn't make these sick feelings worth it. And because I wasn't able to get to sleep properly I woke up tired and cranky. Of course, this is just my experience and isn't necessarily a reliable indicator. But the research is clear on the long-term dangers.

> Energy drinks increase the likelihood of cardiovascular disease, sleep impairment, nausea and nervousness[109].

There are many strategies you can try to increase your energy for work and study. A healthy diet is always better than artificial stimulants.

THINKING OF MENTAL HEALTH ISSUES AS WEAKNESS

In a society where mental health issues are still misunderstood and therefore not fully accepted, it can be difficult to admit your pain to someone else – and to yourself. Speaking up makes you courageous. Speaking up makes you brave.

> One of the great ironies is that admitting you are struggling, or not coping, is actually a sign of strength. It is *not* a sign of weakness.

Being able to recognise what you're going through and communicate it is the first step on the road to recovery. It puts you in a better place than you were before, because you are one step closer to feeling good. Having the conversation with someone else can take a weight off your shoulders. Thinking of stress, anxiety, panic attacks, and so on as weaknesses is not only unhelpful, it's unhealthy.

Pushing your issues to the side and putting on a brave face doesn't make you strong. Pretending that everything is okay is actually detrimental. All it means is that you're mismanaging your health and happiness.

So don't dismiss, ignore or minimise your suffering or the suffering of others. These issues deserve attention and validation, no matter how big or small!

TWD WELLBEING WISDOM

Take time to figure out what *won't* work so that you can instead do the things that *will*.

- **Ask about others' experiences**. Speaking to people who have "been there, done that" can be helpful in learning about what works and doesn't work. Talk with friends, parents, teachers, mentors … whoever you think might help.

- **Research different options**. A quick Google search about energy drinks, for example, will tell you that the dangers of such beverages vastly outweigh the quick sugar hit.

- **Don't be afraid to try different things**. Good health and wellbeing is ongoing; you're allowed a bit of trial and error. I found this with mindfulness … I couldn't get into it. Now I prioritise other things like team sports and reading.

- **Discard any strategies that are unhealthy or unsafe.** Use both your common sense and advice from others. Engage in activities that are healthy and safe!

- **Prioritise long-term gain over short-term gain.** While it's okay to indulge occasionally in guilty pleasures, always put activities with long-lasting benefits first. Going for a run – even though it's hard – is always better than a Netflix binge.

#triggered: knowing what makes you tick

"If I have a dream about my dad [who passed away when I was young], I know I'm stressed because that's my trigger point. I've come to understand that that's my thing," Milly said. "It's important to learn about and understand yourself ... it's difficult, but it's better than bottling it up or finding something like drugs or alcohol to relieve that symptom. Make sure you're exercising, eating healthy, all those things."

Recognising that you need to look after your health and wellbeing is the first step. But where to from there? Try to identify your personal trigger points that might cause you to feel stressed, anxious or depressed. The signs and symptoms can be down to what's going on in your life, and a build-up of pressure over time (such as having too much homework) or having a fight with a parent, partner or friend. Because these issues can hit you at any time, it's necessary to be able to pinpoint your personal trigger points. If you can do this, you'll be better placed to strategically manage and combat it. Everyone gets stressed at some point in time. There's not one person on Earth who has 100% perfect mental health. Knowing what causes your own stress and anxiety helps position you to deal with it head on.

"There's a lot to be said about young people being able to recognise their symptoms and recognise what makes them happy and also what makes them stressed," said Sophia.

"If I have a dream about my dad [who passed away when I was young], I know I'm stressed because that's my trigger point," Milly said.

According to Dr Happy, self-awareness is key. "Reflect on those times when you've felt stressed or got upset about something, and try to identify as early as possible in the sequence of events what started it off, and what were those early reactions. From there, ask yourself what could have been done differently?"

It's helpful to outline some trigger points, so you have a better understanding of what kind of things we're talking about. Below are a handful of my warning signs.

1. I CAN'T GET TO SLEEP AT NIGHT

You will likely be familiar with this one.

I sometimes find that when I get in bed, turn off the light and close my eyes, I simply can't fall asleep, no matter how hard I try. I'll toss and turn for hours, feeling more and more awake with every passing minute, and knowing full well that I'm going to wake up grumpy and irritable the following morning.

This usually occurs in one of two scenarios: either I've got too much on my plate, and the workload is causing me to stress to the point where I can't relax; or, I haven't taken enough time at the end of the day to wind down. Sometimes, it's a combination of the two.

If I'm not sleeping well, I know that I need to take steps to fix this, because as we've seen, a good night's sleep is one of the foundations of optimal health and wellbeing. I'll schedule extra time at the end of the day for relaxation and unwinding, I'll get to the gym so that my body is tired, and I'll switch off all devices long before bedtime.

2. I'M IMPATIENT AND HAVE A SHORT TEMPER

I've always been a pretty mild-mannered person, to the point of being shy for most of my childhood. I almost never lose my temper and it takes a lot for me to lose my patience.

But if I'm feeling stressed or anxious, I tend to snap at people around me, or lose my patience at the most trivial of things. When I become aware of my changing moods, I try to step away from the situation and do something that will put a smile on my face, such as going for a walk in the sun, reading or watching something funny online, or calling a friend. I then look at how much work is on my plate and what can be delegated to someone else or postponed.

3.I CAN'T SWITCH OFF DURING RELAXING ACTIVITIES

Usually, taking a break from work means I unwind, relax and do something fun, often with friends or family. This could be going for a nice bushwalk, or going to the cinema, hitting the pub for a drink or meal, or just reading a book at home or watching some TV. I'm generally pretty good at engaging with these activities and not thinking about work.

But on occasion if I'm out at dinner chatting with a friend, or trying to watch something on TV, I'll find my mind wandering back to the workload, and what emails I haven't yet responded to, or what needs to get done tomorrow … and then I can't enjoy the activity I'm doing at the time.

It's important to switch off and take a break from our work, whether it is homework or study, or a full-time job. In this instance, I find it helpful to turn off my phone, so temptation is out of reach. I also try activities which take me away from the house, so I have a physical separation and therefore emotional distance from whatever's stressing me.

4. MY SKIN STARTS TO BREAK OUT

When I'm really stressed or anxious or feeling under the pump at work, my skin starts to break out and I look like the spotty teenager I was in high school. I never had the worst skin, but I certainly didn't have the best, either. I'd always have a spot or two and it embarrassed me no end. If spots ever come back now, however, it's a sign that my wellbeing isn't where I want it to be.

Taking steps to change this – drinking more water, eating and sleeping better, doing more exercise – have a twofold effect: not only do my stress and anxiety levels go down, but my skin starts to look better again, too. I feel better internally and look better externally!

5. I DON'T WANT TO GET OUT OF BED IN THE MORNING

We've all had mornings where we wake up and can't be bothered. It's so warm beneath the covers. You've got a double period of your least favourite subject that morning. It's raining, and you'd much rather have some quality time with Netflix than go to school.

Anyone who has suffered from severe clinical depression or anxiety will know that the very idea of getting out of bed in the morning is the biggest obstacle that anybody could ever put in front of you. Throwing off your covers when the alarm goes off and putting your feet to the floor seems like the worst idea in the world, because nothing good can come from doing so.

I experienced this feeling a handful of times … and it was always an indication that whatever I was doing to look after myself simply wasn't enough.

If you ever feel you can't get out of bed because nothing good can come of it, then take it as a sign that not only do you need to take better care of yourself, but that you need help doing so. Talk to your family, a close friend, your GP or counsellor.

TWD WELLBEING WISDOM

What are your trigger points?

- **Ask your friends and family**. Those close to you may have noticed things that you weren't aware of … perhaps you bite your nails or change the inflection in your voice when you're stressed. Learning as much about your habits will better help you respond to them.

- **Do research, if you need to**. If you're struggling to recognise your own trigger points, do a quick search online. Identify the ones that sound familiar and jot them down.

- **Develop a plan for when your trigger points arise**. Each sign or symptom of stress and anxiety should be countered with something to alleviate it. Whether that's catching up on sleep, going for a run, eating a healthy dinner or speaking to someone, plan how you're going to respond.

- **Learn what others do**. Many mental health experts, bloggers and advocates talk about what makes them tick and how they respond. Learn from these people.

- **Be powered by your insight**. By knowing your personal trigger points, you are acting proactively. Knowing what makes you tick, and how to respond, will help you stave off any health issues.

Communication and conversation

When I first realised I was sick, I decided that a problem shared was a problem halved. In other words, telling people I trusted about what I was feeling would help me get better.

"The most important contributor to health and wellbeing and longevity and success in life is the quality of our relationships," Dr Happy said.

Speaking about my problems not only lifted a weight off my shoulders, but it gave me insight and perspective into what others thought. In talking about my issues, I was able to lean on other people for support and assistance. This is ultimately what saved me from sinking further.

Being able to openly communicate about what you are feeling – no matter how significant or trivial it might seem – is crucial in managing your health and wellbeing. Talking through the issues allows you to express them in a manner that makes sense to you. It helps you better understand what those issues are, and how best you can tackle them. It clarifies your thoughts.

Speaking up does not have to mean sitting your friends or family down for a dramatic conversation on the couch. You can just write them a text, or send them an email. You can even pen a handwritten letter. It can mean a phone call, where you speak but don't have to show your face. It can mean (if you're sure that's what you want) posting on social media.

I sent an email. I'm much better at communicating in writing rather than speaking, and writing stuff down helped me articulate what I truly thought and felt. For some reason, talking to somebody one-on-one about my issues has been more difficult over the past five years, probably because I feel vulnerable and exposed. Ironically, I find it easy to get up in front of a large group of people and talk about wellbeing in the workplace. These sorts of presentations are a performance and I can put on an act.

Ultimately, find what mode of communication works best for you. In the deepest, darkest stages of my depression, it was late-night emails that allowed me to properly convey what I was going through.

It's also crucial to speak up sooner rather than later.

> "If you've been having a hard time, or you don't quite feel yourself, just tell someone," Chelsea said. "You don't want to wait until it's a big problem, because that's only going to make it harder to resolve."

Talking about your issues helps relieve pressure and will lessen your burden. Keeping things to yourself only increases stress. It doesn't matter how big or small the issue is. Taking the time to talk allows you to share the load. It can be a way to remind yourself that you are not on your own; others will be going through similar, if not the exact same, issues.

"It's a way of connecting and realising that you're not alone, and someone else might be able to empathise. If you don't reach out, your feelings of isolation are going to worsen," Tony said.

Even if you don't have any stressful or anxiety-inducing experiences to talk about, the very act of speaking to your friends is always helpful.

> "If I don't socialise for a couple of days because I'm studying, I start feeling down. I think, 'No-one loves me, I have no friends.' Socialising and being around people is really important," Milly said.

Eileen Condell reinforced this. "Social isolation can cause anxiety, depression, and feelings of worthlessness," she said.

The good thing about getting out of your study cave and speaking to other people is that it forces you to engage with something and someone else than what's going on inside your head. It can make you laugh and stimulate you in ways that your homework and study can't. It's vital for your emotional wellbeing.

> "Having at least one trusted person whom you can go to, who won't judge you, is the first port of call," Mitch Wallis said.

"As long as you have people around you who you can trust, talking can really help. I always like to tell someone that I'm very close to that I might be feeling anxious … I like to talk it through because I'm that kind of person," Alicia said. "Offloading on someone else can help because you're sharing your thoughts, getting a second opinion, but you don't want to let everything out to someone with whom it might turn bad or go the wrong way."

Try to find people of all ages to talk to – you'll learn from their experience and wisdom.

"When I was going through high school, I had a friend who was five years older than me, who I would talk to about other things in the world rather than my studies. It was an opportunity to disconnect from all the stresses," Camellia said. "I had someone to look up to and say, 'Hey, there's a light at the end of the tunnel'. I was fine, I could get through, as others have lived through it."

Sophia found value in mentors. "The way I got through a lot of my issues was having really great mentors, really strong and stable people in my life who had gone through similar things," she said. "I think it was the most important factor in being able to overcome my depression, anxiety and the symptoms of my eating disorder."

Sam D. also raved about the value of mentors.

"The greatest way to learn can sometimes be talking to others who have done exactly the same things: role models and mentors who are not much older than you," he said.

"It could be an older brother or sister, or someone else, whom you can talk quite genuinely and openly with about what worked and didn't work, what they experienced, but most importantly how they managed those darknesses and failures," he said.

Bear in mind that opening up doesn't necessarily mean dumping every single detail in one sitting.

"Sharing your story isn't a matter of blurting out everything and then being done with it – it's a gradual process that takes time," Mitch Wallis said.

When you open up, people may not like what you have to say. That's okay.

As Dr Happy said, "The only way you'll ever really be happy, and be able to develop good relationships, is if you are your authentic self."

Ultimately, as long as you are honest, there is no right or wrong way to talk about your issues. The main thing is you're comfortable and that you do actually communicate with someone – family, friends, mentors, coaches, tutors, medical professionals – because a problem shared is a problem halved.

TWD WELLBEING WISDOM

- **Find a comfortable mode of communication.** Not everybody can talk about their mental health issues out loud. Thankfully, in this day and age, we have email, text, telephone, letter writing … Figure out what works best for you.

- **There is no right or wrong way.** Health and wellbeing is personal. Express what you're thinking and feeling however and whenever you want; it doesn't have to be in chronological order, or even make sense. Just do what feels right.

- **Talk to people you trust.** Choose your audience carefully to make sure you're comfortable sharing personal info.

- **Don't wait too long.** The longer you wait to resolve issues, the harder it is. Telling people who love you early on about what's stressing you out will help you tackle small issues before they become bigger.

- **Talking about anything is helpful!** Even a conversation with friends about your favourite TV show, or sports stars, or celebrities is useful because it allows you to engage with others.

- **Don't isolate yourself.** Connecting with others helps you avoid feelings of worthlessness, depression, anxiety and isolation and keeps you grounded and in touch with the outside world.

Write it down!

"Writing things down is one of the best ways to clarify our thoughts, our feelings and our identity," Dr Happy said.

You may find it hard to say out loud what you're thinking and feeling. That's okay. It's not easy to discuss things that make you feel vulnerable … I find it incredibly difficult sometimes to speak out loud about how I'm feeling.

If talking isn't really your thing, or the idea of it seems too overwhelming at first, try writing it down instead. Writing things down can be a cathartic and helpful experience when dealing with stress, anxiety or depression.

Putting your negative emotions into

written words can help overcome the negativity surrounding it, which can make you feel better[110]. It's the "Bridget Jones effect"[111].

CATHARSIS THROUGH WRITING

When I was sick, I found it impossible to properly express what was going on inside. It seemed weird, embarrassing, shameful, or too heavy for general conversation with my family or friends. Writing things down – in an email, text message or Facebook post – seemed like a good in-between option. I would often do this late at night when I was the most clear-headed. I'd send a message to friends, knowing they might not see it until the following morning. It meant I could express what was on my mind and then go to bed knowing I'd made an effort.

This was a useful process because for most of my childhood and early adulthood I was incredibly shy. Writing was – and still is – the method of communication with which I'm most comfortable. It allows me to say what's truly going on beneath the surface, rather than stammering and blurting out word diarrhoea!

So if painful or stressful thoughts and feelings overwhelm you, and you can't bring yourself to speak about them out loud, try picking up a pen and notepad. Or type it into your laptop, or into the Notes app on your phone. It doesn't have to be an essay; a few words will suffice.

There are plenty of benefits to this process which is known as "affect labelling". It reduces activity in a part of our brain called the amygdala, which is responsible for controlling the intensity of our emotions.[112]

According to Chris Gould, "Journalling can help you reflect, make you aware, and prioritise so that you realise that, ultimately, the senior years of high school are not the be all and end all."

Writing allows you to express how you're feeling in a way that doesn't expose you until you're good and ready. It gives you time to properly consider what's happening, and a safe space in which you can vent. It also leaves a record of what you were thinking and feeling at a certain moment and what might have triggered that.

> Writing things down also helps the brain regulate the emotion that is causing us grief[113]. So, whether you want to keep a diary, or write bad poetry, or think up some song lyrics … give writing a try!

GRATITUDE JOURNAL

You could also try keeping a gratitude journal, or happiness journal.

> Writing down a list of positive events at the close of each day, and why these events made you happy, has been

shown to help lower stress levels and give a greater sense of calm[114].

A close friend of mine, Pat McCabe, introduced me to this idea. A former professional rugby player who played 24 Tests for the Wallabies, Pat was forced to retire from the sport in 2014 after his third broken neck. Having to leave so suddenly, as well as deal with his physical trauma, made for a tough time. Months after his retirement, I was telling Pat about some work issues that were making me anxious to the point of not being able to sleep. He suggested I try a tactic he found useful: keep a notebook on my bedside table and, at the end of each day, write down at least three things that I was grateful for, made me happy, or put a smile on my face. These could be anything, from getting a nice text message from a friend, positive feedback on a task at work, or being able to enjoy a few minutes in the sunshine on my lunch break.

At first, it seemed a bit corny. But what I found was that writing down positive things at the end of each day meant that I was able to remember them. It meant I could turn off the light and close my eyes thinking about positive things, rather than reflecting on negativity. And if ever I was having a bad day, I could flick back through the notebook and remind myself of all the good things that had happened.

"By saying, naming or writing down three things that you're grateful for and appreciate, you can start to build those mental fitness muscles that send positive chemicals to the brain," said Steve Zolezzi.

Louka Parry, an education policy expert, also sees value in this.

"We know that keeping a gratitude journal improves your subjective happiness," he said. "It's important for us to accentuate the positives because people often look for the problems and the negatives, so we need to shine a light on what is right."

A gratitude journal represents a safe zone which can lower your stress levels, make you feel calm at night, and give you a new perspective on what is important to you and what you appreciate.

Try setting aside just 10–15 minutes before bed to jot down a few dot points – set a reminder on your phone if you have to, until it becomes part of your nightly routine, just like having a shower or brushing your teeth.

> It doesn't have to be deep and meaningful. Just make sure it covers whatever has brought light into your day, so you can ensure that light remains bright!

You can do a "happiness jar", for example, where you write down good happenings on scraps of paper, seal them in a jar, and then open up the jar at a time of your choosing. It could be on a day where you're feeling blue, or it could be a momentous occasion, such as New Year's Eve, where you could reflect on all the great things that occurred in the year past.

The gratitude journal worked for me and I'm grateful that Pat told me about it.

You might think that diary writing or journalling is lame. If you're a boy, you might think that it's something only girls do. You might even feel like you do so much writing in school, and then with homework, that the idea of doing even more is crazy!

I've found writing to be a beneficial and cathartic experience. It's enabled me to effectively understand and navigate my thoughts and feelings in a way that I otherwise would not have been able to do.

Not everyone is comfortable speaking out loud about stress and anxiety. If this is true for you give writing a try. You may just find it's what you've been searching for.

TWD WELLBEING WISDOM

"Getting things out of our head and onto paper or your computer, is an effective way to get clarity. From there, it becomes easier to take the next steps," Dr Happy said. Here are a few tips:

- **Schedule your writing for a particular time of day**. Making writing part of your routine will mean you are more likely to do it. I found it useful to write just before going to sleep.

- **Handwrite, don't type**. You may be sick of handwriting after a hard day at school, but I find it more emotionally beneficial to do it the old-fashioned way.

- **Start small**. You don't have to write the next *Harry Potter* ... just a few words describing how you feel (or how you felt) will allow you to reflect.

- **Use your written words as a pick-me-up**: If you're ever having a bad day, scroll back through your gratitude journal and remind yourself of all the good things, even the small ones. They'll bring a smile to your face at a time when you need it most.

- **If you can't speak – write**. Not all of us feel comfortable verbalising how we feel ... especially when we're anxious or depressed. Writing allows us to clarify our thoughts and express ourselves more accurately.

Set small goals

"My self-harm was really hard to get over, because it becomes quite addictive. But I started setting small goals. I tried to get to one week, then two weeks, without doing anything. Eventually it got up to four and five weeks, and then it was months, years."

I had one semester of law school to go when I had my breakdown. I struggled to get through, and felt utterly incapable of doing the weekly readings. My attention span and concentration levels were shot, and the idea of reading an entire chapter for a law subject, or an article, or judgment from a case, was too much for me to handle.

I spent days staring at the tasks in front of me, crying … wondering how on earth I was going to not only do my homework, but also graduate university and become a solicitor. If I couldn't even do the readings, what use would I be to anyone in the working world?

I decided to break the readings down into smaller, more manageable chunks. Instead of trying to read a whole chapter at a time, I would read just one page, or one paragraph. Once I'd completed that, I'd stand up, stretch, have a glass of water, take a victory lap around the house … and then come back and read the next page. Breaking things down made me feel like I was making progress. It helped me feel organised and productive.

Strategies such as this meant that final semester was more tolerable and, together with support from my family, friends and my then-girlfriend, I managed to successfully finish law school and became a solicitor.

A similar thing happened when I was writing this book. As I approached the deadline, I became more and more anxious about how many words I still had to write. At one point, I realised I needed to do 1500 words every day! The thought of writing that many words was nauseating.

But then, one Saturday, I gave myself a four-hour window in which I was going to write. I was aiming for 2000 words. Even someone as terrible as me at maths was able to work out that I therefore was aiming for 500 words an hour.

Suddenly, the task didn't seem so difficult. I reached my goal of 2000 words in just over three hours, rather than four, because I felt calmer and more motivated.

Breaking down those bigger goals by incorporating sub-goals helps make the bigger picture more realistic. It helps you stay motivated – particularly for those tasks that might take a while to achieve – and helps you recognise and celebrate when you've made progress[115].

Small goal setting can also help you get through high school.

Exams and assessments become more and more rigorous as you near graduation. It can feel like there's no light at the end of the tunnel with the mountain of homework and study you have to do.

"School and life can be particularly overwhelming for students – small, consistent steps can make things easier," said Sophie, a careers adviser in a Sydney public school.

When you're assigned an essay for English or history, or a practical task for science, for example, it can feel like yet another burden.

"There's no doubt that accomplishment and achievement are important parts of our satisfaction, important parts of living a good life. If we want to accomplish and achieve, breaking it down and taking things in smaller steps is the best way to do it," Dr Happy said.

Camellia agreed. "When kids are stressed, a task – even the simplest task – can seem like the biggest mountain to climb, simply because of the stress that is associated with it," she said. "But once you break things down into bite-sized pieces, it is so much easier. You realise, 'Hey, I have to write this paragraph and, actually, all of the answers I need are in the book in front of me'."

Flynne found that instead of promising she wouldn't hurt herself ever again, just aiming to get through a single day was more manageable. "My self-harm was really hard to get over, because it becomes quite addictive. But I started setting small goals. I tried to get to one week, then two weeks, without doing anything. Eventually it got up to four and five weeks, and then it was months, years."

If a big goal is too overwhelming and stress-inducing, try breaking it down into smaller goals. Small goal-setting can make a target seem not only more attainable, but also easier to visualise. Saying, "I'm depressed and I want to be happy", or "I'm anxious and I want to be more relaxed" gives you a goal, but it does not offer a pathway to achieving it. It's like saying, "I want to lose 5 kilos in the next 3 months". A clear goal, yes … but with no framework to get there.

Having realistic goals, or targets, is a good way to focus our attention on what is important, or what we need to do. That essay for English class, due in four weeks, is an example of a target we need to meet. But by breaking down that essay into smaller sections, and creating individual deadlines for those sections, we can not only make progress over the course of those four weeks, but we can also save ourselves the headache of cramming the entire assignment in the day before it's due.

TWD WELLBEING WISDOM

How can you set small goals?

- **No sub-goal is too small**. Progress is progress. Even if you only read one paragraph of one page (as I learned to do in 2012), that is still more knowledge than you had before. Break things down in order to get through the work.

- **Celebrate your successes**. Reinforcement is key. Once you complete a task, give yourself a metaphorical (or literal) pat on the back. Feeling good makes it easier to keep going.

- **Less can sometimes be more**. Do little bursts of work frequently, rather than huge blocks infrequently. Incremental progress trumps marathon sessions.

- **Visualise your small goals.** Instead of saying, "I want to drink more water", say "I will drink 4 glasses of water every day". You need to have practical attachment to, and understanding of, the small goals that you are setting for yourself.

- **Be kind to yourself.** Setting a small goal, such as trying to read one page of a textbook at a time, does not make you an idiot or a weak person. This is just a way to help you manage your homework and study as best you can. It worked for me, and it can work for you too.

Take a day off every week

"Elite athletes don't train every day. They train and play hard, but they'll spend just as much, if not more, time recovering, resting and recuperating," said Dr Happy. "We should do the same thing. If you want to be at your best: recover, rest, recuperate."

I suggested to one of my coaching clients that she makes sure she has at least one day off from study and work a week. One day where she can just relax, or go out and have fun, and not worry about her responsibilities. She was confused. A whole day, to just rest and recuperate, she asked? Yes, I replied. One non-negotiable day every single week.

We have a weekend in calendar for a reason. High school students – perhaps more than most – need to switch off and recharge their batteries.

For me, that day used to be Saturday. I had school sport and then usually a party that night. It was a great opportunity to just chill out and have fun before getting back into study on Sunday.

Nowadays, it can be any day of the week, including weekdays (the luxury of being my own boss!). It's important that I have time to do something just for me, whether it's reading a book, having a Netflix binge or hanging out with friends.

My coaching client, having taken me up on my advice, now calls these days "self-care Sundays". You could also call them "mental health days".

With such a hectic study schedule, and with technology making it harder to detach than ever, it's vital we all take the time to simply relax and unwind. If we keep going, every day, at a million miles an hour, we're only going to end up burnt our and depressed.

High school is a marathon, not a sprint, and if we don't pace ourselves, we're not going to do well once we get to those final exams.

Having brief diversions from your homework and study has been shown to vastly improve your focus when you return to the desk[116].

I'm more motivated to do my work if I've scheduled downtime into my calendar for two main reasons: one, it's something to look forward to each week; and two, every time I come back to work after a day off, I feel refreshed rather than tired.

Looking back on her time in Year 12, Sophia said that while she always tried to ensure she had downtime, it wasn't enough. She ended up having a complete crash once she finished her exams. It was a long time until she was able to regain her confidence and motivation to do homework and study.

Now she sees her weekly day off as an opportunity to not only catch up on life admin, but also recharge the batteries. This benefits her wellbeing long term.

"It's just like having a computer switched on every single day for months – eventually that computer is going to crash, because it doesn't have the chance to shut down and reboot," she said.

"Rebooting your engine, restarting your drive, is crucial to your long-term productivity and your mental and physical wellbeing."

One of the best things you can do is take time out – and not feel guilty about it!

"If you do feel guilty, ask yourself, 'Do I want to be productive?' and if the answer is yes, then you need to reboot your engine," she said. "Step back from your homework and responsibilities, and just have some fun … whether it's baking, or going out for brunch, or sleeping in until midday. Experiment with what can make you more productive and relaxed."

Flynne agreed. "When I'm feeling really snowed under, I just need a day to stop and relax, do my own thing, watch a movie, do some knitting. I'm feeling really snowed under right now, actually, so I had a mental health day yesterday. It can be quite proactive in that, yes, you're feeling snowed under, but you're ensuring some time for yourself, and saying you won't continue to magnify this stress, but you'll do something about it."

Spacing out studying by taking breaks in between sessions helps you retain information better than long periods spent with your head buried in the books[117].

You may wonder if you'll have enough time to do your study and homework properly. But by not giving yourself time off to recuperate, you won't be fully focused.

Having a break once a week actually helps you be more productive! So book in a "self-care Sunday", or mental health day, every single week. Give yourself permission to have a day to yourself. You'll be surprised at how much more effective you'll be.

TWD WELLBEING WISDOM

"You can't be 'on' all the time. We need to switch off every now and then, so that you can be on when you need to be," Dr Happy said.

Here are some ideas to help you maximise your time away from homework and study so that when you do come back to the books, you're ready to hit the ground running:

- **Don't feel guilty.** Taking a day off for your mental health is a proactive strategy. It makes you smart, not lazy.

- **Self-compassion is in your self-interest.** Dealing with the stress of high school by giving yourself time off is an investment in your future. It reduces your likelihood of encountering issues down the track.

- **Remember, there is nothing that cannot wait until tomorrow.** You're not a surgeon with a patient that could die on the operating table – you're a teenager! No piece of homework or study is more important than your health and wellbeing … make sure your priorities are in order.

- **Don't expect your day off to cure all of your woes.** It's not a magic solution – optimal wellness requires many things, such as regular exercise and good sleep. Take the day off for what it is … a chance to recuperate, take stock and have some time to catch your breath.

- **Do something different with each day off.** Mixing up the routine of your mental health days will help keep them fresh and exciting. If it's raining, go to the cinema. If it's sunny, go for a walk. Or catch up on your life admin, so that you feel more organised and on top of things.

Detox from technology

"If you limit the number of times you check/respond to [your phone] each day, you limit the constant background noise that's always interrupting and stealing your focus. Instead, each 'checking session' becomes its own concrete item on the 'to-do' list.[118]"

I'm terrible when it comes to my phone and am frequently "that person" who feels the need to check it every couple of minutes, just in case someone has texted or something awesome has happened on Facebook or Instagram (9 times out of 10, nothing has).

I'm sure it annoys my friends. It definitely pisses off my parents.

It can be helpful in staying on top of news and politics. I'm always the first to know about whatever stupid thing Donald Trump has said or done. I like being informed and my phone allows me to keep up with what's going on. But in the long run, it doesn't do my health and wellbeing any good, because I'm always "on", and it's harder to relax and unwind.

When I ignore my phone, or am disconnected from it for some reason, not only do I feel calmer and more at peace, I realise something … I don't need to be so "on" all the time! The world keeps spinning, Trump keeps saying stupid things, and I haven't lost anything.

Even as early as 2010, it was clear more and more kids were going online to solve their problems.

> Seventy-three per cent of teenagers use a range of social networking sites, while 52% have also engaged with blogs and discussion boards of various topics[119].

It's valuable having easy access to resources that you feel comfortable using. Many of you will have sought an answer to a problem via a self-help site, rather than talking to a counsellor or a parent. And that's perfectly okay. Social media can be beneficial. But this doesn't mean that you shouldn't also switch off from technology from time to time in order to protect your mental health.

Detoxing from tech doesn't necessarily mean going cold turkey. "You don't need to delete social media during exams or intense assessment periods to do well; you just need to have self-control and discipline," Sam C. said.

Try it and see how you go. It'll depend on your ability to exercise self-control … if you tell yourself that you're not going to look at your phone until you're finished work, but sneak a glance every 20 minutes, then you're not getting the separation you need to focus. In which case, you need to get serious.

Holly G. took a drastic approach when she was going through Year 12. "I actually ended up getting my mum to change my Facebook password for the last six months of school because I found that it was more stressful seeing all my friends post," she said.

Alicia did the same thing. "I used a few different apps that would lock me out of my phone and Facebook, so that when I was studying I wouldn't have any access or temptation."

This forced separation can be effective. Ideally, we can all be trusted to have a little downtime online, but detoxing completely can work wonders. Ignoring your devices will allow you to better retain information. You're much less likely to remember let alone analyse crucial themes from *Romeo and Juliet* if you're not simultaneously Snapchatting your friends!

Ultimately, doing well at school while staying healthy

and having fun means striking a balance between online and offline.

> "Technology is a weapon that can be used for good or evil. It's not a matter of avoiding it and not using it … it's a matter of knowing how we can use it in the right way – to truly represent who we are and what it means to live a balanced life," Mitch Wallis said.

Using the "settings" function on your phone allows you to turn off notifications, including unread messages in each relevant app. You can also delete random apps that aren't really benefitting you. Go through and unsubscribe from as many useless newsletters and alerts as you can in your inbox, as such junk mail really clogs things up. And set yourself specific times of day when you are allowed to watch TV or movies, so that you know when you're allowed to unwind and when you're supposed to be concentrating.

Some of you might be thinking if you detox from your devices in order to get work done, won't you miss out on all of the fun happening online? Not necessarily.

All of your friends are in the same boat as you; they need to do their homework and study too. So why not suggest to the group that you all have designated times of the day where no one sends any Snapchats, or messages to the group thread, or posts any updates or images, so that nobody has to miss out? And, more importantly, so everyone can get their work done.

TWD WELLBEING WISDOM

- **Switch off all devices 30–60 minutes before sleep.** Winding down, rather than being stimulated by a screen, will help you get to sleep quicker.

- **If you need to – lock yourself out!** We all need discipline sometimes. Take temptation out of the equation by changing your social media passwords and deleting apps until you can trust yourself again or no longer need to be locked out.

- **Keep your phone well away from your bed.** Try leaving it in another room – or at least on the other side of the room – so you're not tempted to grab it to pass the time while you're waiting to fall asleep.

- **Start small.** Going cold turkey might make you anxious you're missing out. Start by not touching your phone for an hour, and see how you go from there. Increase until you feel comfortable being able to take breaks so you can study properly.

- **Have your parents enforce discipline, if needed.** Get Mum or Dad to hold onto your phone during study hours, or ask them to change your login passwords for social media pages.

- **Coordinate detox periods with your friends.** Try scheduling times of day where no one logs onto devices. Strength in numbers!

Exercise!

"Exercise is one of the most potent antidepressants. It's a great stress buster, and associated with fewer and less intensive negative moods, but also more positive moods," said Dr Happy.

After my breakdown in late 2011, I took time to consider what had gone wrong. Why had I developed depression and anxiety? I was angry with myself for having allowed my health to deteriorate. Looking back on the two previous years, I saw things I was doing to make myself unwell, but also what I wasn't doing. Most striking for me was the fact that I had stopped doing any exercise.

I had such tunnel vision about my workload at university, my part-time jobs and my volunteering commitments that I had given up doing the things that I loved most: playing team sports and reading books. Both physically and emotionally, this made my health and wellbeing worse. Once I made the connection, I re-joined my old social sports teams, I started walking every day, sometimes several times a day, and I got back into the gym.

It's been one of the best things I could have done. And I'm not alone in this.

More sport and exercise equals less depression![120] Exercise increases your energy levels, helps you maintain a healthy weight, prevents osteoporosis, and later-in-life illnesses like cancer or heart disease.

> Something as simple as a nightly walk after dinner will improve your wellbeing and quality of life[121].

Jogging, swimming, cycling, walking, dancing and even gardening all reduce anxiety and depression[122], improving your self-esteem and cognitive function[123].

According to Dr Jenny Brockis, "Studies have shown that people who exercise on a regular basis do better academically. Physical activity gets more blood pumping to your brain, bringing more oxygen and nutrients so you're primed to study more effectively. In addition, it helps to burn off stress, boosts mood and increases the release of our feel-good hormones. Sitting for too long makes it harder to think, learn and remember."

Regular exercise is crucial not only for your health and wellbeing, but also your ability to focus and study. Incorporate proper exercise into your routine, but make sure you also have quick, scheduled breaks during the day. For example, get up every 20–30 minutes for a walk around the house; stop to have a glass of water; go outside for a minute for some fresh air … Moving around as much as you can while studying will keep that blood flowing to where it needs to be!

You may worry you won't have any time left in the day to do your homework or study, or that you'll be too tired once you come back to the desk. But what I have found is that exercise not only makes me feel more energised, it also makes me more productive. It has the opposite effect as it reduces your anxiety sensitivity and propensity for panic attacks[124].

> Students who exercise or do sports after school score lower for depressive moods than students who don't[125].

Regular exercise helps structure your day. While it might seem like you won't have enough time to get everything done, a structure actually helps motivate you to maximise your study time.

"It was good to have structure where I'd have sport training in the afternoon, then I'd go home and do an hour and a half of work, then have dinner, rather than just going home and saying, 'I have to work all evening'," Alicia said.

> "Exercise can help with time management. If you go home and

you've got the whole night to study, you might put it off. But if you exercise at some point, you've got to allocate your time better, and therefore you'll be more productive," said Sophie.

Exercise won't fix all your problems but it's critical for your health and wellbeing. Take the time to figure out what form of exercise might be best for you and incorporate it into your daily and weekly schedules. Here are some options.

TEAM SPORTS

I love team sports. From an early age, I played cricket and soccer, then added track and field in high school. These days I'm involved in at least two different social sporting teams each week; usually a rotation of indoor soccer, mixed netball and touch football.

Team sports give me so much: I can sweat out any stressors and it's a great opportunity to hang out with my friends. In fact, schoolboy cricket games on Saturdays with the guys are some of my most treasured high school memories.

Because of its social nature, team sports have better health benefits than individual activities[126].

"Young people who are regularly engaged in physical activity have been shown to have lower levels of depressive symptoms and stress, and higher levels of psychological wellbeing and health-related quality of life," said Pree Benton.

If you don't go for a solo run, or a gym session, you're only letting yourself down. But if you skip training or a game with your team, you're letting down a whole bunch of people. Since we're social creatures, this can provide an additional layer of motivation to ensure that we get our exercise done.

RUNNING

Going for a run is a simple, convenient and cheap way to get your exercise fix. You don't even need to go anywhere in particular; just run around the block and through your neighbourhood streets at any time of day.

"I liked to go out for runs in the mornings before school, because it woke me up and set the tone for the day," Alicia said.

Running helps relieve stress because it boosts serotonin, which creates more positive moods. It sharpens your focus and mental stamina, boosts your immune system and fitness levels, reduces cholesterol and burns calories. And – as a result of all this – it makes you look better! What's not to like?

On an emotional level, running provides a sense of freedom, it allows you to control your own destiny as you can go as fast or slow as you like, set your own timing goals and milestones.

It can also be a great social activity – joining a running group, or forming one with your schoolmates for before or after class, can be a great way to make new friends.

WALKING

If running is too strenuous, try walking instead. It has all the same benefits as running, such as endorphin rushes and increased focus and stamina, as well as decreasing stress and improving sleep and self-image. Whether you walk slowly and gently or fast and vigorously, you're going to get physical and therefore mental health benefits.

> Walking in nature can lead to lower risk of depression[127], given its marked difference from life inside with your head buried in textbooks.

The only problem with walking, however, is that your mind can wander back to your workload. What I like to do is put on my headphones and listen to music or a podcast. This gives me something to focus on and it can be a great way to accomplish two relaxation activities in one go.

You might be better at switching off than me! In which case, walking and listening to nature can be a soothing experience and one which can help put into perspective all that's going on in your life.

SWIMMING

Despite being one of the driest countries on Earth, we Aussies love the water. As we get older, however, it can become less about physical activity and more about sunbaking for those hot Instagram shots. This is certainly the case for many adults (myself included).

> Swimming – whether in the ocean or a pool – offers a range of physical and mental health benefits. It improves lung capacity (and therefore our breathing and heart health) and is one of those rare all-body workouts that gets all of your muscles and joints moving.

Emotionally and psychologically, it is a meditative exercise, which forces you to concentrate on powering up and down the pool, or through the waves. Water can have a calming effect on your state of mind, and provide a literal and physical disconnect from everyday life.

As with running, it can be a great way for you to set goals and challenge yourself by timing your laps or doing more each session. Such milestones will give you a sense of accomplishment and make you more confident and enthusiastic when you next have to hit the books.

YOGA

The ancient Indian philosophical practice of yoga combines physical postures, breathing exercises and meditation. It's a low-impact activity with minimal risk of injury, and it can be done by people of most ages and at any level of fitness. Depending on what kind of class you take, it can vary from gentle and accommodating to strenuous and challenging … it's very *flexible*!

Yoga can reduce the impact of stress and levels of both anxiety and depression[128]. It's a self-soothing activity, through which you can meditate, relax, exercise and even socialise with you friends[129].

It can also influence other response systems in the body; it can reduce heart rate, lower blood pressure, aid your breathing, and assist the body in responding to stress in a more flexible fashion[130].

> Yoga can play a protective and preventative role in maintaining levels of mental health and wellbeing[131]. It can have both immediate and long-lasting benefits in reducing anxiety[132].

Yoga can be a great social activity. Get a bunch of your mates together to attend classes, either before or after school, or go by yourself and meet a new circle of friends. Once you're reasonably proficient, you can practise yoga pretty much anywhere – at home, at the beach, in a park. Wherever you want.

HITTING THE GYM

The great thing about gyms these days is that there's something for everybody. You can use bikes, cross-trainers, treadmills and rowing machines if you want to do high-intensity cardio. You can do stretching and core workouts. Or you can lift weights (with supervision).

High-intensity and resistance training delivers multiple mental health benefits. Not least, your susceptibility to depression is greatly reduced.

> In addition to getting fit, specific training at the gym can help relieve anxiety, improve cognition and memory, increase self-esteem, and aid healthier sleeping patterns[133].

Of course, you might not like working up a sweat ... and there's nothing wrong with that. But the good thing about physical activity and exercise is that there are endless ways in which you can do it – not everyone has to join a touch football team or be a yoga guru.

> "If you don't like exercise, you have to weigh your distaste for squat-thrusts against your distaste for saddlebags.

> Negative thinking got you all fired up? Great, take that motivation to the mat! Committing to an exercise plan is a hell of a lot easier than wallowing in self-destructive behaviour and crippling depression.[134]"

"Exercise can mean going to the park and throwing a Frisbee with your mates, or kicking a soccer ball around, or surfing. Whatever works for you, so long as you get the body moving for a certain amount of the day or week," said Dr Happy.

Even if you don't like being active, trust me that it's good for your physical and mental wellbeing. Find something that works for you and make it a regular part of your routine!

TWD WELLBEING WISDOM

Exercise has been proved to help manage psychological distress, anxiety and depression, and even prevent such issues from arising in the first place. Given the stressful nature of high school, exercise in ways that suit your personal needs and interests. Here are some tips:

- **Make time, don't find time**. I know it can be hard finding time for physical activity. Blocking out space and writing it in your diary makes it more likely that you'll be able to do it, as opposed to just hoping you'll have a spare hour.
- **Choose a time of day that suits you**. You might be a morning person, you might be an evening person. Figure out what time of day is best for you and try to exercise at that time as often as you can. Forcing yourself out of bed early won't be motivating or inspiring for you if you function better in the PM!
- **BUT ... don't exercise too close to your bedtime**. Physical activity too close to lights out can keep us awake. As with our use of devices, stop any exercise 30–60 minutes before bed so that our bodies can unwind and prepare for sleep.
- **Allow sufficient rest time between exercise**. While physical activity has many health benefits, too much can also be detrimental. Our bodies need time to recover, especially from high-intensity workouts. Give yourself adequate rest so that when

you next exercise you'll be able to get the most out of the session.

- **Make your exercise a social affair**. Working out is more fun with others. Ask a friend or family member to join you on a run, walk or gym session – you'll be able to have a good chat as well as getting your exercise fix. A training partner can also be a great source of motivation for you to actually get out of the house and get physical.

- **Combine exercise with other pleasures**. Listing to music, podcasts or audiobooks while exercising can be a great way to ensure you switch off from the stresses of school. It also allows you to kill two birds with one stone.

- **Don't be too hard on yourself**. There will be times where you feel too snowed under, or tired and unmotivated, to exercise. That's okay. It's near impossible to maintain the ideal weekly routine all the time. Be kind to yourself and just stick to your routine as often as you can; you won't lose any ground if you miss a workout or two.

- **Have fun!** Exercising can be tough, especially if you push yourself hard. But ultimately it should be something you do because you want to and because it gives you pleasure. Allowing yourself to enjoy it will make it easier for you to switch off and forget about your homework and study commitments.

Tuning out with mindfulness and meditation

"Whatever phase of life you are in, make time to pause and reflect where you are heading. It is a good time to insert a comma now and realign yourself to your inner self before your life ends in a full stop.[135]"

In late 2016, a primary school in Baltimore in the US took a new approach to discipline. It replaced detention with meditation.

The Robert W. Coleman Elementary School decided that, instead of punishing naughty kids by sending them to the principal's office, taking away their play time or giving them detention, they'd be instead sent to a "Mindful Moment Room" – a safe space filled with lamps, decorations and pillows. Here, children would undergo breathing and meditative practices, calm down and discuss what incident led them to being there.

The results were stunning – at the time the US media picked up on the story, the school was reporting a total of zero suspensions for the two-year period since they'd started the program.

This "reactive" strategy to address student issues is a real success story. But meditation doesn't have to exist solely as a substitute for punishment; it can also be incorporated into our school day or as a relaxation technique for when we're at home[136].

"One of the most important things students can do, to ensure they remain engaged, is find ways to switch off. Even just 10–15 minutes of meditation a day can make a big difference," said Peter.

Doing mindful activities for as little as 10 minutes each day can bring about small changes in your levels of resilience and wellbeing[137].

As I mentioned, I don't get much out of meditation. I can't turn my brain off for long enough and focus. I get my fix from other activities, like team sports or reading books.

But that doesn't mean that mindfulness and meditation won't work for you. Plenty of people – including those whom I interviewed for this book – rave about zoning out to meditate. The failure here is mine, not that of the activity itself!

"Mindfulness gives students a tool to manage anxiety, and also understand, accept and manage their emotions. It's a way of being able to become aware of things, being able to ground yourself in your body and give you the ability to regulate your emotions so you can feel them but don't need to act on them," Nicola said.

Aside from meditation, the recent craze for adult colouring books delivers a similar result. Both psychologists and publishers have started targeting people of all ages who are seeking new, cool ways to clear their minds and cope with difficult emotions. Colouring books may be the answer!

While colouring, you are engaged in a structured activity that – unlike a lot of what you do at high school – isn't goal-oriented. Colouring shifts your focus onto something manageable and less stressful[138]. It might seem like a simplistic, easy activity. But that's precisely the point.

By taking a break from your study to engage in a deliberately simple activity, you will be better placed to deal with your work once you come back to it. Taking a mental time-out with some textas or pencils can help set you up for whatever challenges are on your desk. And the very act of creating something pretty and colourful has a beneficial effect, too[139].

You might first try it out of nostalgia – it could remind you of your childhood – but there are proven benefits.

Taking my own advice, I went and bought a colouring book and some textas. I gave it a go one evening after a long day of work. Part of me wanted to just turn on Netflix and be a sloth, but I thought I'd try it out. The first page in the book was a peacock, which I thought would be a good challenge. I used every coloured texta in the pack to create a pretty ugly looking bird, albeit a very colourful one. Next thing I knew, 45 minutes had passed and I hadn't thought about work that entire time. Both the knowledge of that, and the physical sensations of colouring, made me feel a whole lot better.

By engaging in a mindful activity that took my energy and attention elsewhere, I had successfully switched off from work and recharged my batteries.

"If you've got five minutes to trawl Facebook, you've got five minutes to meditate.[140]"

Nicola Lipscombe, who founded Powerful Listening, said that eating your lunch at school, running around, or kicking a football can all be mindful activities.

"The idea is to be fully focused on what you are doing and being aware of that. If it's a football, for example, you pick it up, look at it, feel it, bounce it … you're aware of where your body is in space and you focus on your legs, feet and the way you're looking into the distance for the goal and how your foot connects with the ball. That's a mindful practice," she said.

In other words: we can create our own mindful moments in our everyday activities. Be aware of your movements and thought processes so that you can switch off from stress and reflect on what you think and feel.

You can be mindful in almost any situation, really.

Playing with your dog, drawing, painting, watering your plants, going for a drive, sitting outside, doing a jigsaw puzzle … it's up to you!

Practising mindfulness as a high school student increases your level of calm, relaxation, self-acceptance, emotional regulation, awareness and clarity[141].

Research shows that mindfulness practices can decrease symptoms of depression and anxiety[142] and, interestingly, bring about greater levels of trust in your friendship group[143]. It's also been shown to improve your focus on personal goals, and help sustain your attention with homework and study[144].

"If you've got five minutes to trawl Facebook, you've got five minutes to meditate. It's not that we don't have the time; it's that we give our time to other things. It's a critical tool we can use to start to slow down and start to escape that cult of business that we are all caught up in.[145]"

TWD WELLBEING WISDOM

Here are some tips to get your started:

- **Find an app**. Guided meditation and mindfulness apps teach you how to sit and control your thoughts and breathing for short stints, increasing to longer periods.
- **Or… choose an activity that forces you to concentrate**. Colouring in is good, as it requires you to focus on your pencils or textas on the page, and nothing else.
- **Set a convenient time**. Since it is supposed to relax you, mindful or meditative activities should be done when the time is right.
- **Find a suitable location**. Find a spot in which you feel calm. It might not be at the desk you've been working at all day … try a neutral space.
- **Start small and slowly**. Try it for just a few minutes first. It's better to get a 2–3-minute meditation right, rather than a 10-minute one half-heartedly.
- **Let go of "all or nothing" thinking**. You can't solve every problem with a few minutes of calm, nor will you have an out of body experience. Focus on what needs to be focused on, and have reasonable expectations.
- **Be patient**. These practices are hard to master but they're like a muscle – the more you work at it, the stronger it will be.

Practising positivity every day

"Positive psychology is not 'happyology'. It's not about being happy all the time. It's about being able to embrace all of life, and all of your emotions, in a balanced way. We are negatively wired, and thus run a negativity bias. We look for threats and danger more so than we look for the good. Positive psychology helps us redirect a little bit," Nicola Lipscombe said.

We're living in an age of environmental uncertainty. Global warming, an increased threat of terrorism, and a whole range of social, political and cultural issues confront us every day. On top of this, rates of psychological distress, anxiety and depression are rising, especially in young people. If you're going to be able to deal with this stuff, you need skills and strategies[146].

This is where positive psychology comes in.

What is positive psychology?

> "[Traditional] clinical psychology is reactive. We wait until people fall off a cliff, and then we try to pick them up. Positive psychology is more about putting a fence up at the tip of the cliff. It's about prevention," Dr Happy said.

As the name suggests, positive psychology aims to alleviate the negatives in life by promoting the positives[147], helping people thrive by building on their strengths and virtues[148], and emphasising wellbeing, flourishing, character, meaning and purpose[149].

It's not about looking at what's wrong in our lives and trying to fix it. It's about identifying what is right, what works, and leveraging that. This approach is useful both for people who are unwell, and those who want to get ahead of the game.

What does this mean for you?

Earlier in this book, I spoke about the need to create and

maintain a stable table-top. To keep that table-top steady and in place, you need to make sure you have multiple legs … one for study, one for friends and family, one for sleep, and so on. The more legs you have, the more stable your table-top – and your health and wellbeing.

A 2011 study showed that, on average, school students who participated in a positive psychology program in their classes performed 11% better in tests than students who didn't[150]. Why? These sort of programs promote the positive elements of student life, such as uplifting emotions, resilient mindsets and optimistic character[151]. Your school might already have similar programs on offer. If that's the case – awesome! Ten points to Gryffindor.

But you can also take individual responsibility for yourself and do your own positive practices. Everyone's different, so just do the exercises and activities that work best for you.

DOES BEING POSITIVE MEAN BLOCKING OUT THE NEGATIVE?

Absolutely not. As much as they suck, negative experiences are an integral part of life because they actually teach us how to learn and grow. If we never experienced anything bad in our lives, we wouldn't be able to properly appreciate the good!

American author Mark Manson maintains that negative emotions are normal and healthy – in fact they're necessary to maintain happiness! You just need to express them in a safe and acceptable manner that aligns with your values[152].

"Because we are automatically always scanning our environment for threats, we need to compensate by deliberately and intentionally balancing that out with what is good about life and what is good about the world," Nicola Lipscombe said. "We need all the emotions. But we don't need to be living with a constant fear response, which is what a lot of students are living with now."

We're not trying to eliminate or ignore the things that are going wrong. Instead, we're trying to approach them in a way that highlights what is good, so that we don't get bogged down in what is bad.

I'm pretty cynical by nature. If 99 out of 100 things go right, I'm more likely to focus on the one thing that went wrong. But when I force myself to redirect my attention to the stuff that went well, it's easier for me to feel optimistic and proud.

WHAT ARE SOME POSITIVE PRACTICES I CAN TRY?

Practising positivity doesn't mean forcing yourself to be happy, or putting on a brave face if you actually feel like crap inside. It's simply about highlighting what is good and valuable and meaningful in your life, bringing out the happiness within yourself.

So how do you do it?

In an earlier chapter (**Write it down!**), I spoke about the benefit I got from keeping a **gratitude journal**. The act of jotting down three things, each night, that I was grateful for helped me better remember all the good things that were happening in my life. As a result, I was also better at not getting caught up in any stressful things, and I could always go back and read over the good things when I was feeling bad.

But **expressing gratitude** does not necessarily just mean

keeping a journal. You could keep a **happiness jar**, which holds all of your good memories and can be opened at any time. You can also express gratitude in person or over the phone with your parents, friends, partners, or whomever you want. It's the act of acknowledging what you appreciated that day – from having a roof over your head to being given a compliment by someone – that will help you connect to more than just your individual experience. You could take photos of the things you're grateful for (if they're tangible), or share your thoughts via text message. There are countless ways.

Try **savouring each moment**. This means giving all of your attention to a pleasurable activity as it happens, consciously allowing yourself to enjoy the experience[153]. For example, if you're watching a movie or TV show on Netflix, don't be on your phone at the same time. Just have fun watching! Otherwise, you won't get as much out of it.

Schedule time for a **productive pause**. With life moving at such a frantic pace it's crucial to know when to simply disengage. This is just as important as knowing when to engage. Pausing allows you to ask yourself what, how and why you're doing what you're doing. It'll give you the time and space to reflect on how best to proceed, instead of crashing headfirst into a brick wall[154].

"Whatever phase of life you are in, make time to pause and reflect where you are heading. It is a good time to insert a comma now and realign yourself to your inner self before your life ends in a full stop[155]."

Random acts of kindness can be hugely beneficial. These can be done either at school or outside of it. It might mean helping a friend or teacher walking down the corridor carry their heavy bags, or giving someone 50 cents so they can buy something from the school canteen, or sharing your study notes with a friend who is struggling with a particular class.

These little, random gestures obviously help the other person, but they're also great for you too. "It's actually a way of connecting and strengthening relationships, which are key for resilience and wellbeing," Nicola Lipscombe said. Random acts of kindness are infectious, and being kind to others reminds you that you too need to be kind to yourself.

Surround yourself with positivity. We are influenced by the people we spend the most time with, whether that's our parents, siblings or teachers. But we can choose our friendship circle. Try to surround yourself with people who are optimistic, inspiring and kind, rather than those who are competitive or bitchy.

Develop a daily self-love. Even spending as little as 10 minutes doing something that feels good, and brings you joy, will help you carry a sense of calm and balance through the rest of the day. This can be anything from meditation to push-ups to watching cat videos on YouTube … if it puts a smile on your face, or makes you feel better (and it isn't unhealthy!).

Finally, **leverage your strengths**. This means identifying what you're good at and applying it in your daily life – even if it doesn't come naturally to you. If you can't think what your strengths are (or you are at a point where you're unable to see what you're good at), ask the people in your life who know you. I know I'm a good listener, so I get my mates to talk to me about whatever is going on in their life, so I can best help them.

Practising positivity really can help with your physical and mental wellbeing. It can help you academically too, because it helps you cultivate greater empathy, altruism and social behaviours. These skills can have long-term benefits for your career success and job satisfaction[156]. We all flourish when we are positive. It sure beats letting negativity take over!

TWD WELLBEING WISDOM

Positive psychology helps build your resilience so you can manage life's ups and downs. Here are a few tips:

- **Practising positivity does not mean ignoring negative thoughts and feelings**. Stuff goes wrong and there's nothing we can do about it. Denying the bad only makes it worse. Part of positivity is facing those negative experiences head on, so you can learn and grow from them.

- **If you're not able to find positives, seek help**. We all have our bad days. But if you're at a point where you're unable to see the good, and you can only see the darkness … speak with someone: your parents, teachers, school psychologist, or read the Resources chapter.

- **Practise gratitude in your own way**. Figure out a way to show gratitude that is consistent with how you live your life

- **Allow time for reflection**. One of the cornerstones of positive psychology is allowing yourself the time and space to consider where you're at and where you're going. Make time, don't find time for this.

- **Practise positivity in conjunction with exercise, reading, and all the other activities you do**. There are positives to be found in most everything you do if you look hard enough!

Listening to escape

If you catch the bus, train or ferry, you'll know that just about everybody is looking at their phones and wearing headphones.

You might think they're all caught up in their own worlds, taking no notice of anyone else. But there's at least one good reason why people may be doing this: they're listening to something fun, relaxing or informative and it's good for their health.

MUSIC

"Listening to music can help increase your happiness during tough times, as your mind is a muscle and can be retrained to positive thinking patterns," said Amba Brown.

I've always been a huge classical music fan. Thankfully it also turned out to be a great study companion. Classical music can be soothing and calming. I can't listen to music with lyrics while studying, though, because I can't stop myself singing or humming along!

Playing music has been shown to help your wellbeing, and improve your mood over time[157].

Music can also be a helpful indicator for our moods, as – according to Dr Happy – many people will select songs based on how they're feeling. "It helps you feel like you're not alone," he said.

When I'm angry, a bit of death metal is perfect. When I need calm, I go for classical. And when I'm driving, something to sing along to is always the best.

You'll also come across songs that seem to speak to you whenever you're in those moods. Musicians have the power, sometimes, to put into words what many of us struggle to say out loud.

The band Linkin Park really spoke to me as a teenager whenever I was feeling down or overwhelmed; songs like "Crawling" and "Easier to Run" were awesome in getting me through. Lead singer Chester Bennington's suicide in mid-2017 hit me hard, as it brought home to me just how real his lyrics were.

There are a bunch of current artists that you may find speak to you on a level you need in times of hardship. Lorde, Ed Sheeran, Sam Smith, Demi Lovato, Paramore and Imagine Dragons – among many others – have produced anthems that can help people through the tough moments.

In Newcastle, New South Wales, Headspace run the Yarn Safe project, through which students of Aboriginal and Torres Strait Islander descent have had the opportunity to write, perform and produce music[158]. What quickly became clear was that music allowed students the opportunity to express any stress or anxiety from school, relationships, home life, and so on, they were feeling.

"When I'm a bit down, I listen to one of my favourite songs, or one of my rappers; it gets a smile on my face and I sing to it," one of the students told ABC Newcastle. "I like singing, but I don't know if I'm really good at it. I just sing all the time, so [when I heard] there was an opportunity to do it, I was like, 'Yeah, I'd love to do this'."

Both Natalie and Rachael, parents in Perth and Brisbane respectively, had similar results with their kids, who had always loved playing and performing music.

"We put a turntable in [my daughter's] room and she would

play classical music, or jazz, or whatever it was that she loved, while she was studying. I did often wonder if that was the best and most effective way to study, but that was the way she needed to do it in order to deal with the stress and anxiety," Natalie said.

"[My son] played the clarinet and the drums, and it was really helpful for him because he really enjoyed those activities. They were a different outlet for his energy, and helped him connect to people," Rachael added.

Whether playing yourself, or simply listening to it, music can positively impact your emotions and motivate you, by making you feel happy and improving your mood[159].

PODCASTS, AUDIOBOOKS

In the past few years, I've really gotten into podcasts and audiobooks. You can listen to comedians, history and documentaries, true crime, news and politics … there's just so much variety. They demand your attention, though. Music allows you to tune out while listening … but with the spoken word, you have to concentrate. This is crucial for me, as switching off is often difficult. Being taken to another place – whether it be real or imagined – doesn't just allow me to disconnect; it forces me to.

"I found that listening to *Harry Potter* [on audiobook] has helped," said Milly. "It takes me back to a place of happiness and childhood. I don't have to be completely focused, because I know the story, but it's another voice that gets me outside of my head. I'm not thinking of everything that I have to do. I found that if I fall asleep to that, then I'm not going to sleep stressing." Don't listen to podcasts or audiobooks while you're trying to study, though. The spoken word will only distract you! Use them as a way to redirect your attention to something more relaxing, to help you disconnect, in a study break or day off. And vary the podcasts or audiobooks depending on your mood. Stand-up comedy at night can help you wind down from a stressful day of reading and note-taking. Or perhaps a murder mystery will distract you from whatever you have on the following day.

"There's something for everyone, no matter what you're interested in, whether it's astrophysics or philosophy or politics or comedy," Dr Happy said. "If you can be intellectually and socially stimulated, that's a good thing."

TWD WELLBEING WISDOM

Listening to music, podcasts or audiobooks is a great way to shut out the stresses of daily life and escape into another world.

- **Create different playlists, artists or episodes for different moods**. In need of relaxation? Play music you find calming. Want to put a smile on your face? Listen to a comedy podcast. In need of something uplifting? Try some motivational songs, or positive reinforcement podcasts. Determine what you need for each mood, and have playlists ready to go.

- **Find people to play with**. Making music with others is a great way to not only switch off, but also feel connected[160]. Form a band with your friends and get together regularly to jam.

- **Share your music, podcast and audiobook recommendations**. If you've benefitted from something you've listened to, share it around … they'll respond in kind.

- **Don't listen while studying if it affects your concentration**. Just as lyrics distract me, work out what will keep you focused and what won't.

Pick up a good book and read!

In the 18th century, English essayists Joseph Addison and Sir Richard Steele wrote that, "Reading is to the mind what exercise is to the body[161]."

While we now know that exercise benefits more than just your physical health, curling up with a good book is not only enjoyable, but it's great for your emotional and psychological wellbeing, too.

You don't need to be reading for too long before you get some benefits – even just six minutes can help reduce muscle tension and slow down your heart rate. Reading for 30 minutes every day can help relieve longer term stress[162].

You might be turned off by the idea of reading as a way to unwind, given how much you already have to read for homework and study. But just imagine being transported to another place, another time, another state of mind. When it comes to activities that calm you down, help you de-stress and relax, reading is – for me – one of the best.

A good book demands your attention and leaves no wiggle room to be checking your phone. I've always found sitting down with a book and blocking out everything else helps me unwind and feel better about my life. I read old favourites like *Harry Potter*, Agatha Christie's Hercule Poirot murder mysteries or John Marsden's *Tomorrow, When the War Began*. These books take me back to times and places where I had few worries, responsibilities and experiences. A time of innocence, unbridled joy, and security.

Carving out at least half an hour a day for reading is a non-negotiable aspect of my routine. But there are other reasons to read as well.

There is mounting evidence of the dangers of staring at screens all day – particularly at night before you go to sleep. Watching a movie on your laptop or devouring social media on your phone can really mess with your sleeping patterns.

I love reading just before going to sleep. Even thirty minutes helps my eyes adjust and not feel strained.

Reading can reduce stress levels by up to 68%[163], and is 700% more likely to help you relieve stress than playing video games[164]!

Why is reading so effective? Like mindfulness and meditation, the brain must be fully focused on the single task of absorbing whatever is on the page. This helps you switch off, thereby reducing stress and enhancing relaxation. Reading is more than a simple distraction – by engaging with the words on the page, you stimulate your creativity and enter what is, essentially, an altered state of consciousness[165]. Diving into a good book can also help you become more empathetic and increase your self-awareness. It can improve your relationships with others and increase your understanding of them[166].

Being able to empathise will help you be kinder not only to others around you, but also to yourself. You'll feel more comfortable in your own skin.

"Reading is a form of relaxation, but it's also intellectual stimulation, as it takes us into different worlds and makes us feel connected at the same time," Dr Happy said.

Regular reading throughout your life has been shown to increase your mental capacity and improve brain health in old age. If you keep your brain engaged through books, you are far less likely to experience a decline in cognitive function[167]. Reading helps you not only maintain your mental health as a teenager ... it has flow-on effects for your life as an adult and a senior citizen.

You may worry that reading might make you appear socially awkward, or lonely, or isolated from your friends or classmates, because it is a solitary activity. I have three responses to this: one, reading does not have to be the only way in which you try to manage your wellbeing – you can still play team sports or go out and see friends as well.

Two, reading fiction in particular increases your connections with those around you[168], because your increased empathy with and understanding of characters helps you better relate to others.

And three, even if the first two didn't exist, there is no reason why reading cannot be a social activity. Set up a book club with your friends. You can have organised catch-ups, hang out away from homework and study, and still get all the benefits.

Whether it is improved brain function, reduced stress and anxiety, a welcome distraction and opportunity to escape to another world, increased empathy and social understanding, broader vocabulary, a chance to be mindful or even just a way to save some cash (by not going out), reading is a fantastic way for you to switch off from the rigours of homework and study and enjoy some personal time.

Think about it … reading Harry Potter for the hundredth time might actually make you healthier and happier! What more can you ask for?

TWD WELLBEING WISDOM

"Unless you're always inside reading a book and avoiding life, there's no downside and no side effects," Dr Happy said.

- **Treat reading like mindfulness and meditation**. Reading makes your brain focus on a single task.

- **Reading before bed helps you sleep**. Unlike your phone or laptop, reading books – even on a Kindle – won't expose you to bright lights. Schedule reading time and disconnect from devices.

- **But you can also read at any time of day**. Whether on the bus or train, during your lunch break, or late at night, you can pick up a book anytime you want.

- **Read for at least 30 minutes a day**. Despite your busy schedule, carving out half an hour isn't too difficult. It will break up the rest of your day and help as you head to sleep.

- **Form a book club**. Books become even more enjoyable when you're able to share the experience. Why not get a group of friends together to meet once a month?

- **Escaping to another world doesn't mean distracting yourself from actual issues**. Losing yourself in a novel actually helps you deal with any wellbeing problems you might be facing, as it reduces stress, anxiety and improves brain function.

Netflix binges . . . and other guilty pleasures

"Everything that is pleasurable in life will kill us a little bit, but nothing will kill us faster than not having any pleasure," said Dr Happy.

Every now and then, just do nothing.

Day-to-day life has never been faster. Technological advancements mean that working professionals can get tasks done from home, respond to client emails remotely, and effectively never leave the office. For high school students, social media means you can stay up to date (literally, to the minute) with our peers.

Given all this, it's crucial to simply do something lazy and indulgent every now and again! Flopping onto the couch to watch episode after episode of a TV show, for example, will help us slow down, take stock and escape.

I love nothing more than re-watching old Disney movies, bingeing on whatever new Netflix show is dominating newsfeeds, or going back to old sentimental favourites such as *The West Wing* (my highbrow guilty pleasure) or *Geordie Shore* (my very, very lowbrow one).

Milly agreed that vegging out can be crucial for your wellbeing. "I would come home from being at the library all day, having done a solid amount of work, and just veg in front of the TV," she said. "I decided to reward myself, which I found was a really good way to unwind, relax and not go to bed thinking about things, because I'd have enough time to let it all go."

"'Me time' is a right, not a privilege. Sacrificing your hobbies on the altar of the must-do list is no good. They should be on the must-do list to begin with. You have to consider your hobbies – and the benefits you get from indulging in them – to be as important as the other stuff you 'need' to do.[169]"

I can feel guilty if I'm not doing anything with my time. This becomes even more pronounced if I'm not doing anything that you'd call "productive". But I've learnt that if I push too hard, I burn out. If I don't allow myself time to unwind and de-stress, my stress and anxiety becomes greater.

One major benefit of having suffered from anxiety and depression is that it gives me an insight into what I can and can't do. Knowing what I now know, I feel strongly about not allowing myself to get overwhelmed, frazzled or fragile.

Allowing myself time off to just laze about in track pants and a hooded jumper (or my onesie, if I'm feeling particularly indulgent), eating junk food and sipping tea is very important in helping me to get back to basics and be a kid.

It's a common temptation. Occasionally it can be beneficial to give in to it and just enjoy some quiet time with hedonism and entertainment. Many of you might be reluctant to have such guilty pleasures; you may, ironically, feel guilty for doing so.

"Too many students feel guilty for taking time out to just read a book, watch TV or do something purely for pleasure, but self-care is a really important practice to maintain good psychological wellbeing," Pree Benton said.

It doesn't have to be watching Netflix. Find whatever indulgent activity helps you relax. Don't be afraid of enjoying such pleasures from time to time … doing so not only allows you to have more fun in your schedule, but also gives you perspective on how hard we sometimes push ourselves and, as a result, what's important.

> Milly said, "Having time where you switch off is a really, really important thing, because if your mind is constantly 'on', then you're just going to explode."

TWD WELLBEING WISDOM

Imagine a life without indulgence. Boring, right? "It's perfectly fine to engage in some non-productive, or even unhealthy, behaviour at times (so long as it's within limits)," according to Dr Happy.

- **Be self-compassionate**. Don't feel guilty for doing something indulgent every once in a while. Let go if and when you need to.

- **Keep perspective**. Binge periods are acceptable, but be mindful. Acknowledge your Netflix splurge, or night on the couch with chocolate, for what it is … a way to recharge.

- **Downtime is important**. We can't always be "on". Eventually, we need a break. Allow yourself that break when you need it, unwind accordingly, so that you can be more productive.

- **Guilty pleasures are more fun with others**. It's great to binge on TV, or eat junk food, but it's even better with friends.

- **"Switching off" means switching off!** Turn off your devices … or at least put them in another room. Make the most of your downtime.

Counselling, medical assistance and medication

"I didn't want to be that person who had to rely on medication. But, as so many people kept telling me, if you've got diabetes you have to take your meds."

Everyone around you will, at some point in their lives, experience a mental health problem. Or they'll know somebody whose mental health has suffered, or is suffering. For some, this might be as mild as elevated stress for a short period of time. For others, more serious issues will arise, and you will need time, treatment and good support to recover[170].

You might not want to seek professional help from counsellors or psychologists, or consider taking medication. I can appreciate why. But be open to the possibility … it could be just the thing you need.

It can be scary to think about sitting in a counsellor's office, or taking anti-depressants. Why? Both scenarios will be accompanied by having an actual diagnosis for what you've been going through – meaning you have a recognised problem[171].

Instead of thinking of this as a negative, think of it as a positive: if you can pinpoint what is happening by analysing your experiences, signs and symptoms, you will be better placed to manage it. And effective management of our wellness requires us to be proactive.

SEEKING PROFESSIONAL HELP

"Seeing a psychologist means you are ready to just be you – in whatever state that might be. It's like having a personal trainer at the gym; you need someone to spot you so you can lift the weights, especially if you're carrying an injury.

That's not a sign of weakness, it's the road to success," Mitch Wallis said.

Going to a psychologist was one of the first things I did when I realised I was sick. Having an objective professional to talk to, who could offer a neutral perspective, was something I was really keen to explore. It also offered a kind of security blanket, as I knew there was a safe space available if my friends or family were unable to offer advice … which happened on a number of occasions.

You may be hesitant to seek support from a counsellor, psychologist or psychiatrist for a number of reasons. You might feel ashamed or embarrassed and fear what others will say about you if they knew. You might feel like you are already equipped to deal with any issues. You might have trouble identifying what signs and symptoms mean you should seek professional help, rather than relying on yourself and others[172]. Or you might feel a sense of hopelessness and think there no one can possibly help you[173].

But there are many benefits to be had from seeking professional help. Your emotional confidence and mental health literacy will be stronger[174], and your capacity to manage any issues will be better.

For Sam C., seeking help from a psychologist was the turning point. The psychologist's guidance helped make his path to recovery seem less overwhelming.

"Some form of professional support outside of your friendship and family networks is invaluable when it comes to managing your wellness throughout high school," he said.

"Secondary students today are facing greater levels of stress and anxiety than ever ... professionals – such as your school counsellor or on-site psychologist, who are bound by confidentiality – can move mountains in confronting these challenges."

Alicia had a similar experience, although she wished she had sought help earlier.

"I got professional help about three or four times [when I was getting close to final exams]. If I'd done that a bit earlier, it would have been more helpful because – even though it was great having my parents' opinions and support, and close friends' as well – it was nice to have a professional perspective on what was going on," she said.

Parents will see the value in getting professional help, especially when there are issues beyond your control.

"[Our daughter] was seeing a psychologist on a regular basis when she was going through Year 12. We got to the point where we realised we couldn't help her with particular things, such as self-harm. We could help her so far, but she needed somebody outside of the family to talk to, and not feel afraid," Tony said.

"Counselling and psychology services are really important if you get to the point where you are not coping, regardless of what that looks like."

I'm glad I decided to seek professional help. I couldn't have gotten through without it.

MEDICATION

"I'm a huge advocate for medication. The stigma of it turning you into a robot doesn't happen like how they show it in the movies," Mitch Wallis said.

I was reluctant to take anti-depressants for my depression. I felt strongly, to the point of stubbornness, that I could handle my health problems without that crutch (ironic, since I had no problem seeing a psychologist). I thought I was smart enough to recognise what was wrong with me, and take steps that would make me feel better.

Eight months after my initial breakdown, however, I changed my mind.

The box-ticking approach that I had tried was not working. This only served to compound my frustration, as it seemed like I was losing more and more control with each passing day.

Eventually, I realised that taking medication did not mean that I wasn't able to look after myself; it just meant I had a safety net. It meant I was doing everything I could to boost my mood and wellbeing. It meant I was using all necessary measures to help keep on the road to recovery.

Taking medication didn't mean I was weak. It meant I was not only strong enough to do what needed to be done to be healthy and happy again, but that I had a security blanket.

Some of you might feel you'll become reliant on medication, or that you'll lose control of your health and wellbeing. While anti-depressants do stabilise your mood, your doctor will help you come off them at a suitable speed. You will, once again, be able to regulate your own thoughts and feelings without that added assistance.

"I was on medication [while at school] and I feared that I was going to become reliant on it, and I didn't want to … so I went off it," said Milly. "But this year, I again set too many expectations for myself, goals that I couldn't possibly meet, and I felt overwhelmed and I crumbled again.

"I still refuse to accept that anxiety is just something that I have, that I can't always control. It's so frustrating. I didn't want to be that person who had to rely on medication, but as so many people keep telling me, if you've got diabetes you have to take your medication."

I don't see a psychologist anymore; I haven't done so for about two years. But I still seek help from family, friends, mentors, colleagues and coaches. I recognise and appreciate the need for external advice and guidance from people I trust, and am comfortable with the idea that there may again come a time where I need to seek professional medical advice. There's nothing wrong with that.

And I haven't taken medication for more than four years now. I'm pleased that I'm at a point where I can support myself without having my mood fluctuate throughout the day. But I know that, if and when I ever need medication again, it won't mean I'm not strong or that I have failed. It's just a reflection of what I might need at that point in time in order to function at the level I want, and to remain productive and successful.

TWD WELLBEING WISDOM

I am not suggesting you *must* take medication, or seek professional services. Just be open to it if suggested by your GP, or a friend or family member. Always bear in mind that:

- **Find someone who you feel comfortable with.** Choose a counsellor or psychologist with whom you have a rapport. Don't waste time (and money!) on someone who you can't open up to.

- **You are being proactive.** Good management of our health and wellbeing requires us to take whatever steps are necessary. Congratulate yourself for taking this particular step.

- **Professional help does not make you helpless.** Seeing a counsellor is just one way to look after your wellness. For an hour a week, you are in someone else's hands; otherwise, you're in charge.

If advised to take medication, remember the following:

- **Meds don't make you weak.** Nor does it mean you can't look after yourself. It's just a way to help you get through each day.

- **Mental illness is no different to other ailments.** You wouldn't begrudge someone using medication to manage cancer. Anxiety, depression and other mental illnesses are no different.

How can I help others who are struggling?

"For many teenagers, their first approach will be to a friend. Don't be afraid to ask the simple question, 'are you okay?'" Dr Happy said.

You may not suffer from any mental health issues. But there will be people around you who do. They might be family members, friends, classmates, and even your teachers. Lending a helping hand is one of the kindest things you can do. Here are some ways you can assist those around you.

REGULAR COMMUNICATION

> "You don't have to be a psychologist, psychiatrist or teacher. You're just a friend. Check if there's anything you can do to help, let them know you're there," Dr Happy said.

If you sense someone is stressed or anxious, encourage them to confide in you. Provide a comfortable environment for them to do so. Whatever form of communication that works for you may not necessarily work for them. For example, I find it useful to write things down, whereas others may find it easier to just have a chat. Let the person know that you can communicate with them in whatever way suits them best. Doing so will make them more likely to open up. If the person does confide in you, there are a few things to remember:

- Listen and don't interrupt;
- Be kind and sympathetic;
- Be firm, where necessary, but never aggressive;
- Promise confidentiality, and keep that promise (unless the person is at risk of harm);
- Offer whatever practical support you can.

"Connecting with someone who is experiencing a mental illness is the number one way to reduce stigma and increase their connection to a community," Mitch Wallis said.

SHARE YOUR OWN EXPERIENCES

"Empowering individuals to tell their story is going to be therapeutic for them when it's done in the right way. That has to start with people who have been through it to stand up and lead by example," Mitch Wallis said.

In the course of my work, I often get to travel around Australia, giving lectures and workshops to law firms, universities, community organisations and schools about mental health issues. In a lot of presentations, I discuss my personal experience with depression and anxiety, how it all started, how I got through it and where I'm at now. I tell my story both as a cautionary tale and also to give a message of hope: if I can get through it, so can you.

Following these presentations, I often receive emails from students and lawyers saying how much it meant to them to hear what I'd been through, and that listening to me speak helped them realise what action they need to take to again be healthy and happy.

My favourite example of this came in late 2015, when I got a message from a student at the University of Technology, Sydney, saying that hearing me talk had encouraged her to open up to her parents about what she was going through. Having the courage to do this was the first step on the road to recovery.

> "As soon as somebody else starts talking about their own stuff, it just makes it so much easier for others to start being honest and opening up," Sophia said. "I think that's a big issue in addressing self-stigma; if others speak, you feel more comfortable."

You don't need to have suffered from serious issues to be able to inspire your friends. Share an example of a time when you felt overwhelmed, or anxious, and tell your friend how you managed. Or, just tell them about how you sometimes feel that way, and how much it sucks for you.

Hearing of others' experiences can be helpful to those suffering. It will allow them come to terms with whatever is going on inside them, and make them more comfortable opening up in return.

PARTICIPATING IN ACTIVITIES

The reality of helping others is that, sometimes, people

won't respond to even your best efforts to get them to talk. Instead, infer what they might need and encourage them to get involved.

> "One-on-one chats can be confronting for young people, so engage them with activities that don't require talking," Alicia said.

I'm a big team sports person. Getting back into indoor soccer, mixed netball and other games really helped me and my recovery. And I was more motivated because of the opportunity to do an activity with others. If you don't go for a solo morning run, you are only letting yourself down. If you miss a game of sport, you are letting down a whole team of people. Since most of us hate letting others down, it can be hugely motivating to try doing group activities.

If you are helping someone who's suffering mental health issues, encourage them to join you for runs, or walks, or a game of touch footy … whatever it might be to get them to physically engage. Like me, they might feel inspired to do the activity so as to avoid disappointing anyone else.

BE SYMPATHETIC TO THE UPS AND DOWNS

It's highly likely that the person you're helping will have times where they go backwards. Having depression is not like having a cold; it is not a linear process. As such, progress towards recovery can often be undone by one bad moment or interaction that sets a person back.

Anyone who has ever experienced anxiety or depression will tell you that, sometimes, the idea of getting out of bed and putting your feet on the floor is the biggest obstacle that anybody could ever put in front of you. At times like these, having people around who care for them is crucial. Be kind to them if they're having such a day. Acknowledge the setbacks for what they are, and help them get back on track.

ENCOURAGE THEM TO ENGAGE RESOURCES

Some people may not want help. They may be embarrassed to talk about their wellbeing, or too proud, or just not know how. If you can't get through to them, gently suggest they speak with a counsellor or psychologist who can offer more objective solutions and strategies. Be prepared. They might not respond positively to your encouragement; in fact, some people may react with hostility.

"One girl in our class got extremely anxious during exams to the point that it was distracting other people. Another classmate said to her, 'I really think you should see a counsellor', and she got offended by that," Alicia said. "I totally understand this, because it's hard to hear that you should go and see someone and not get offended. It's quite a sensitive topic, and reveals that they could be vulnerable."

If they react badly, remember two things: one, you suggested they get help for a reason; and two, their safety and wellbeing always takes precedence over the potential for disagreement.

Be comfortable suggesting external help if the situation calls for it. It may require you to break the confidence of a person (which you should only do in extreme cases).

About four years ago, one of my best mates from school was struggling with depression. Feeling as though my advice and that of others was no longer having an impact, I called his dad. While his dad was already aware of his son's problems, I felt like I was breaking his trust. Ultimately, I decided that the safety of my friend was more important than anything – even my friendship with him. He could have cut me off forever for what I did, and that was a risk I took because I cared so much for his wellbeing. I'm very pleased to write that he did eventually recover, and is currently healthier and happier than I've ever seen him.

TWD WELLBEING WISDOM

One of my greatest pleasures since recovering from depression has been helping others. I wouldn't be where I am today without the help of family, friends and mentors. Giving back in some small way is the least I can do in return.

- **Stay in close touch**. Feelings of isolation are par for the course with psychological distress, anxiety and depression. Let the person know that they're not alone by contacting them regularly, even if it is just a simple text message to say hi.

- **Share to help them open up**. We all draw inspiration from anecdotes that we can relate to. Encourage openness by vocalising your own struggles.

- **Gauge the situation and act accordingly**. There will be times when a person needs you to be sympathetic, and other times where they need you to suggest action. Strike the right balance between what you think is best and what they need in that moment.

- **Break confidentiality only when necessary**. People who confide in you about mental health issues deserve your utmost respect and trust. But their safety is critical – the moment you feel like nobody around can help, or you fear they might self-harm, get help, whether that's from someone's parents or a medical specialist.

- **Get involved in activities that will help them**. Helping others requires more than just conversation, it also requires action. Get the person out of the house for a walk, or a movie, or invite them to a social gathering. They are more likely to participate if you are there to guide them through.

- **Allow them to have bad days**. There is no "one size fits all" solution to mental health issues. People will have periods where they crawl back into their shell, no matter how much progress has been made. Be kind when someone regresses, allow them a moment, and then get them back on the horse.

- **Suggest resources that will help them specifically**. If your friend is tech-savvy, they might appreciate online forums which offer confidential support. If they can only talk to someone face-to-face, help them find a counsellor nearby.

- **The advice you offer others is the same advice you should give yourself**. One of the great ironies of mental health issues is that, often, we are good at telling others what they need, but when faced with the same issues ourselves, we choose to ignore them. If roles were reversed, your friend would want you to listen to the advice they were offering you.

- **And** … don't ever give up on someone. You wouldn't want them to give up on you.

Resources

"Recovery can't happen until you say, 'I'm ready to get help,'" Mitch Wallis said.

Logging onto the Internet and seeking mental health support was not the done thing when I was in high school – such resources weren't available, nor were mental health issues as widely discussed or recognised. Today, students are flocking online for assistance that is not only convenient and easily accessible but also confidential, anonymous and immediate.

"I used a lot of [online resources], which were really helpful when I had moments of distress and couldn't necessarily run to someone about them," Flynne said. "It was easy to just log on and say, 'This is what I'm feeling, can you please help me', and they can give you some strategies right away."

Sixty-eight per cent of young people say online resources help them work out what they need, 70% say such resources make it easy to seek help, and 64% say the online sphere helped them better understand their experiences[175].

High school students face many barriers when it comes to accessing support for mental health issues – stigma, cost, transport, waiting times, and so on – and as such online resources are invaluable. Ninety-seven per cent of students surveyed who identified as LGBTQI said online services provided them with a safe and supportive community. One-third came from regional and remote areas, and of that group approximately 16% said they had not sought help prior to going online, despite feeling or knowing that they needed help[176]. According to ReachOut, 1.31 million young Australians access its digital services.

As I say, online resources would have been really helpful for me. As someone who is competitive and prone to perfectionism, I would have found it useful to use an online service without anyone else knowing.

While I support openly communicating with your friends and family about whatever issues you might be going through, I appreciate that many people do not feel comfortable doing so. If this sounds like you, then seek help from online resources. And if you're not comfortable using apps or websites, there are plenty of reputable hotlines to call, many of which run 24 hours a day.

The resources listed here range from government-funded bodies to start-up platforms. As noted in the Disclaimer at the start of this book, my listing them here does not mean I think you need to try any or all of them. As always, consult with your GP, counsellor, psychologist or psychiatrist about what may be best for you.

APPS

Appreciate a Mate (free – positive affirmation)
In need of positive reinforcement? This may be the app for you. Founded by the Young and Well Cooperative Research Centre, it lets you send or share affirming messages and quotes to friends and family, with customised pictures and colours. Images can be saved or shared on social media, so the message of positivity can be spread far and wide.

Black Dog Snapshot (free – self-assessment)
Whether you're in need of professional help or not, it is important to keep track of your health and wellbeing. This app gives you an overview of your wellness levels over time, including a tracking of your general happiness and stress, social support and even alcohol consumption. Significantly, it also provides feedback on Australian norms, based on your age and gender.

BoosterBuddy (free – mood tracking)
This app helps you track your wellbeing levels through a series of daily quests designed to create and maintain positive habits. It also helps you stay on top of your daily schedule and increase social interactions.

Breathing Zone ($6.99 – mindfulness)
One of the simpler and easy to follow mindfulness apps, offering guided breathing exercises to slow your breathing rate, calm you down and help you feel more relaxed. It's not cheap, but it's worth it.

The Check-in App (free – helping others)
Developed by beyondblue, this platform allows young people to develop a strategy to help their friends. It takes the fear out of having a conversation with those around you who might be struggling, and provides building blocks to looking after their mental health.

Daylio (free – mood tracker)
A private diary in which you don't have to type a single line! By collecting and recording your moods and activities, you will be able to better understand your habits and what creates different moods across the day, thereby allowing you to form better habits and be more productive.

Headspace (free or $12.99/month – meditation, mindfulness)
A gym membership for the brain! The Basics pack will teach you how to meditate with guided episodes of as little as 10 minutes per day. Further subscriptions will give you access to hundreds of meditations on everything from stress and anxiety to sleep and focus.

iMood Journal ($2.99 – mood tracker)
Using colourful charts, note pads and even hashtags, this app aims to help you understand the connection between your moods and experiences. It's a personal diary that tracks

everything from sleep, medication, signs and symptoms, energy levels … the works.

Moodnotes ($3.99 – cognitive behavioural therapy)
This app utilises the principles of CBT to help correct behavioural patterns that lead to negative thoughts and feelings. At different intervals during the day, the app will ask, "How are you?" and you answer by rating your mood with a range of emoticons. Follow-up questions help get to the core of how and why you are feeling a certain way. Tracking your mood as such allows you to better understand your wellbeing patterns and how best you can tackle different situations.

Pacifica (free – cognitive behavioural therapy, meditation, mindfulness)
Featuring psychologist-designed tools to address your stress, anxiety and depression, this app aims to break the cycle of mental health issues using tools that specifically target negative thinking. You can progress through the steps at your own pace. Paid versions are also available.

Panic Relief (free – anxiety, stress, panic attacks)
Using a range of animations, this app helps you cope with the triggers and symptoms of panic attacks, allowing you to feel calm and in control, and eventually overcome the fears that might have caused such an attack in the first place.

PAUSE ($2.99 – mindfulness)
A mindfulness game which incorporates ancient Tai Chi practices, in which you move a blog that looks like lava around a screen – slowly and with precision – until the blog grows big enough to cover the whole screen. You'll then be prompted to

close your eyes and savour your sense of calm before getting back into work. A quick way to calm down.

ReachOut Breathe (free – stress and anxiety)
Using your smartphone's camera, this app allows you to monitor and control your breathing and heart rate in real time, so you can actively address the onset of physical stress symptoms such as shortness of breath or a tightening of your chest.

ReachOut Worrytime (free – anxiety)
If you're not able to switch off from your worries, this may be the app for you. It allows you to file away your concerns until a certain point of the day, so that you don't have to agonise over them all the time – you can come back to them later. It then helps you review those worries and discard them if they are no longer relevant.

Sleep Cycle (free – sleeping patterns)
Given how troubled our sleeping habits can be as teenagers, it is important that our REM cycles be as uninterrupted as possible. This app tracks your rest patterns and awakens you with its alarm clock at the moment when your sleep is at its lightest, allowing you to get up in the morning feeling more refreshed than you otherwise would be.

Smiling Mind (free – meditation)
One of the more popular mindful meditation apps, this platform is starting to sweep schools across the country through its addition to curriculums. Developed by renowned Australian psychologists, there are different courses to suit each age group.

Stigma (free – anxiety, depression, bipolar disorder)
Rated as the number one app for mental health at the time of writing, this platform helps you build a support network by journalling what's on your mind and keeping track of your mood. A paid version is also available for $2.99/month.

Talkspace (free – on-demand therapy)
FaceTime therapy? Sounds good to me! Talkspace offers therapy sessions via video chat or text within 24 hours of request, which is perfect for those who are in need of counselling but cannot get an appointment for days if not weeks. Pricing starts at approximately $25 per session, depending on your needs and length of discussion.

Thought Diary Pro ($7.99 – cognitive behavioural therapy)
This guided journal helps you record and change the thoughts that cause emotional and psychological distress by identifying "thinking errors" and challenging the thoughts and beliefs that cause you grief. By facing your negative emotions head on, you can change their destructive ways.

Worry Watch ($2.99 – anxiety)
By journalling and logging your everyday activity, this app helps you analyse your perceptions of what *could have* happened in scenarios versus what *actually* happened, thereby challenging your preconceived ideas and anxieties, which can help us frame a more positive outlook.

WEBSITES

batyr (batyr.com.au)

A youth-based, charitable organisation that aims to empower young people by removing the stigmas surrounding mental health issues like depression, eating disorders, and alcohol abuse, among many others. batyr normalises these issues by addressing the proverbial elephant in the room, and by encouraging active participation in the reduction of health problems. It has gained widespread national recognition, such as through its promotional campaign with one of Australia's super rugby franchises, the NSW Waratahs.

BITE BACK (biteback.org.au)

For kids aged 12–18, this site promotes positive psychology for young Australians with blogs, stories and mental fitness challenges.

Black Dog Institute (blackdoginstitute.org.au)

Most of us will be familiar with the animated video of a large black dog following people around. The Black Dog Institute provides multi-media educational programs on depression, and other psychological illnesses, as well as effective treatment strategies for those suffering from psychological distress. Self-help tests and downloadable materials are also available.

Butterfly Foundation (thebutterflyfoundation.org.au/web-counselling/)

The most prominent service for young people suffering from eating disorders, disordered eating or body image issues. Run by professional counsellors, it offers live, one-on-one counselling between 8.00 am and 9.00 pm on weekdays.

The Desk (thedesk.org.au)
Aimed primarily at tertiary student health, wellbeing and support, this site provides information, self-help content and community forums. It is run by the University of Queensland, with support from BeyondBlue, and can give you a great insight into life as a university student.

Graeme Cowan – I am Back from the Brink (iambackfromthebrink.com)
Graeme Cowan is a former corporate bigwig who suffered with depression for years. He also attempted suicide on multiple occasions. He is now an international author and public speaker known for empowering people and helping them overcome depression. In addition to his website and books, he also has material available on YouTube and Facebook.

Happify (happify.com)
A range of engaging games and activities to measure wellbeing and build happiness. For anyone over the age of 16.

Headspace (headspace.org.au)
Headspace is a government-funded organisation that provides mental health counselling, education, employment, and alcohol and drug abuse assistance. The website also provides a significant range of online and downloadable resources that cater to an individual's personal needs.

The Lowdown (thelowdown.co.nz)
This Kiwi website has a simple slogan on its homepage: "straight up answers for when life sucks". Sounds good to me!

mindhealthconnect (mindhealthconnect.org.au)
An online portal providing mental health information, along with information from a wide range of online services, for people of all ages.

Out & Online (counselling for LGBTQI persons – outandonline.org.au)
Set up for Australia's LGBTQI community, this nationwide service offers early intervention assistance for people aged between 18–25, all hours of the day.

ReachOut (au.reachout.com)
My personal favourite. Australia's leading youth mental health and wellbeing website for people aged 14–25, with fact sheets, stories, forums and apps to help young people understand and manage their mental health.

SANE Australia (sane.org)
SANE conducts innovative programs and campaigns to improve the lives of people living with mental illness – family and friends. It also provides a helpline and website, both of which contain thousands of contacts from around Australia.

SuperMe (playsuperme.com)
A gaming and online resources platform aimed at teaching and building resilience, self-esteem and positive thinking.

YouthBeyondBlue (youthbeyondblue.com)
A site which aims to empower young people aged 12–25, as well as their family and friends, to respond to depression and anxiety in the most productive way possible.

HOTLINES

Butterfly Foundation (eating disorders)
1800 33 4673
The most prominent service for young people suffering from eating disorders, disordered eating or body image issues. Run by professional counsellors, it offers live, one-on-one counselling between 8.00 am and 9.00 pm on weekdays.

Drug & Alcohol Counselling (alcohol, smoking, drugs)
1800 888 236
Available 24/7, this service is for those who are struggling with mental health issues either caused by, or which give rise to, excessive consumption of alcohol, drugs or smoking.

Gay and Lesbian Counselling and Community Services of Australia (LGBTQI)
1800 184 527
Depending on what State you're in, the phones will be operated between 5.30 pm–10.30 pm or from 7 pm–10 pm.

Kids Helpline Chat (personal and physical safety)
1800 55 1800
Aimed at kids aged between 5–25, this service runs 24/7, every day, and is also online.

Lifeline Crisis Chat (depression and suicide ideation)
13 11 44
Offers short-term support for people who are overwhelmed or having difficulty coping with issues and struggling to feel safe. It is aimed at persons aged 15 and older and has staff answering the phones between 8 am and 4 pm.

MensLine Australia (mental health support for males)
1300 78 99 78

A professional online and telephone service for males of all ages to help deal with relationship problems and other mental health issues, as well as provide information and other referral services. Open 24/7.

QLife (counselling for LGBTQI persons)
1800 184 527

Aims to keep sexual minority communities connected. Its telephones are staffed between 5.30–10.30 pm.

Suicide Callback Service
1300 659 467

A 24/7 telephone service available to people over the age of 15 who are experiencing suicidal tendencies, and/or are at immediate risk of suicide. This service is especially helpful for people in remote or regional areas.

TWD WELLBEING WISDOM

There is not necessarily a right or wrong answer when it comes to seeking help for your health problems. But there are several things I would definitely recommend:

- Be open to suggestions from all trusted sources. Why? Well, because even an outlandish idea may hold the key that unlocks the mystery solution to your struggles.
- Remember that people who help you do it out of the kindness of their hearts. In other words, do not dismiss or ignore those who are genuinely trying to help.
- Try not to expect to be miraculously cured overnight … these things can take time.
- Also, don't assume that by taking steps towards recovery your problems will automatically be solved … it is not a matter of ticking boxes.
- There is a greater spiritual commitment to managing your wellbeing that you need to address.
- Make sure that you take the time to reflect on the progress you are making. Keep a diary, debrief with a friend, family member or classmate … or meditate or pray … whatever works for you.
- Lastly, acknowledge how far you have come.

Congratulate yourself on taking steps in the right direction. Asking for help is not an easy thing to do; but it's something that you will never regret.

Endnotes

1. Australian Institute of Health and Welfare (2011), *Young Australians: their health and wellbeing*, 2011. Cat. no. (PHE 140), Canberra: AIHW

2. Kessler, RD et al (2005), Lifetime prevalence and age-of-onset distributions of DSM-IV disorders in the National Comorbidity Survey Replication. *Archives of General Psychiatry*, 62: p. 593–602.

3. Slade T, Johnston A, Teesson M, Whiteford H, Burgess p, Pirkis J, et all (2009), *The Mental Health of Australians 2: Report on the 2007 National Survey of Mental Health and Wellbeing.* Canberra: Department of Health and Ageing.

4. Manson, M "5 things that should be taught in every school" (online), 20 July 2015 <https://markmanson.net/taught-in-school>

5. Ibid.

6. Australian Institute of Health and Welfare (2011), *Young Australians: their health and wellbeing*, 2011. Cat. no. (PHE 140), Canberra: AIHW

7. Kessler, RD et al (2005), Lifetime prevalence and age-of-onset distributions of DSM-IV disorders in the National Comorbidity Survey Replication. *Archives of General Psychiatry*, 62: p. 593–602.

8. Leonard et al, *Private Lives 2: the second national survey of the health and wellbeing of gay, lesbian, bisexual and transgender (GLBT) Australians* (2012), Australian Research Centre in Sex, Health and Society, La Trobe University, Melbourne.

9. Slade T, Johnston A, Teesson M, Whiteford H, Burgess P, Pirkis J, et all (2009), *The Mental Health of Australians 2: Report on the 2007 National Survey of Mental Health and Wellbeing.* Canberra: Department of Health and Ageing

10. BeyondBlue, "Signs and symptoms", date unknown <https://www.beyondblue.org.au/the-facts/depression/signs-and-symptoms>

11. The National Institute of Mental Health, "Child and Adolescent Mental Health: Overview", date unknown <https://www.nimh.nih.gov/health/topics/child-and-adolescent-mental-health/index.shtml>

12. SANE Australia, "Is someone you know unwell?", date unknown <https://www.sane.org/mental-health-and-illness/facts-and-guides/is-someone-you-know-unwell>

13. Cooke, K (2013), *Girl Stuff*, Penguin Random House Australia, p. 254

14. Templeton, L, "Why I'm embarrassed to tell people I struggle with depression", *The Mighty*, 22 August 2017 <https://themighty.com/2017/08/embarrassed-of-depression/?utm_source=newsletter_mental_health&utm_medium=email&utm_campaign=newsletter_mental_health_2018-01-05>

15. Black Dog Institute and Mission Australia (2017), *Youth Mental Health Report – Youth Survey 2012–2016* <https://blackdoginstitute.org.au/docs/default-source/research/evidence-and-policy-section/2017-youth-mental-health-report_mission-australia-and-black-dog-institute.pdf?sfvrsn=6>

16. Australian Bureau of Statistics (2007), National Survey of Mental Health and Wellbeing: Summary of results. 4236.0, Australian Government, Canberra

17. Black Dog Institute and Mission Australia (2017), *Youth Mental Health Report – Youth Survey 2012–2016* <https://blackdoginstitute.org.au/docs/default-source/research/evidence-and-policy-section/2017-youth-mental-health-report_mission-australia-and-black-dog-institute.pdf?sfvrsn=6>

18. Ibid.

19. Australian Institute of Health and Welfare (2011), *Young Australians: their health and wellbeing*, 2011. Cat. no. (PHE 140), Canberra: AIHW

20. Kessler, RD et al (2005), Lifetime prevalence and age-of-onset distributions of DSM-IV disorders in the National Comorbidity Survey Replication. *Archives of General Psychiatry*, 62: pp. 593–602.

21. Slade T, Johnston A, Teesson M, Whiteford H, Burgess P, Pirkis J, et all (2009), *The Mental Health of Australians 2: Report on the 2007 National Survey of Mental Health and Wellbeing.* Canberra: Department of Health and Ageing

22. Templeton, L, "Why I'm embarrassed to tell people I struggle with depression", *The Mighty*, 22 August 2017 <https://themighty.com/2017/08/embarrassed-of-depression/?utm_source=newsletter_mental_health&utm_medium=email&utm_campaign=newsletter_mental_health_2018-01-05>

23. Lawrence D et al (2015), *The Mental Health of Children and Adolescents – Report on the Second Australian Child and Adolescent Survey of Mental Health and Wellbeing.* Canberra: Department of Health.

24. Australian Bureau of Statistics (2016), *Causes of death*, 2015 Cat. no. 3303.0. ABS: Canberra

25. Dyson et al, *Don't ask, don't tell. Report of the same-sex attracted youth suicide data collection project* (2003), Australian Research Centre in Sex, Health and Society, La Trobe University, Melbourne

26. Black Dog Institute and Mission Australia (2017), *Youth Mental Health Report – Youth Survey 2012–2016* <https://blackdoginstitute.org.au/docs/default-source/research/evidence-and-policy-section/2017-youth-mental-health-report_mission-australia-and-black-dog-institute.pdf?sfvrsn=6>

27. *Raising the bar for youth suicide prevention*, Orygen – The National Centre of Excellence in Youth Mental Health, 2016 <https://www.orygen.org.au/Policy-Advocacy/Policy-Reports/Raising-the-bar-for-youth-suicide-prevention/orygen-Suicide-Prevention-Policy-Report.aspx?ext=.>

28. Ibid.

29. Dunn, M (2016), *Letters to Mitch*, self-published, pp. 192–194

30. Slade T, Johnston A, Teesson M, Whiteford H, Burgess P, Pirkis J, et all (2009), *The Mental Health of Australians 2: Report on the 2007 National Survey of Mental Health and Wellbeing.* Canberra: Department of Health and Ageing

31. Arboleda-Florez, J (2002), "What causes stigma?", *World Psychiatry*, 1(1) pp. 25–26

32. Cowan, G (2013), *The elephant in the boardroom: getting mentally fit for work*, via <http://graemecowan.com.au/product/elephant-in-the-boardroom-getting-mentally-fit-for-work/>

33. MediaCom Melbourne (2015), *Youthbeyondblue Anxiety and Depression Ad Tracking Survey Post Campaign Research*, p. 7

34. Black Dog Institute and Mission Australia (2017), *Youth Mental Health Report – Youth Survey 2012–2016* <https://blackdoginstitute.org.au/docs/default-source/research/evidence-and-policy-section/2017-youth-mental-health-report_mission-australia-and-black-dog-institute.pdf?sfvrsn=6>

35. Ibid.

36. Ibid.

37. Ibid.

38. Holsman, J (2016), *The High School Survival Guide*, Mango Media, Inc, p. 151

39. National Eating Disorders Collaboration, "Eating disorders in schools: prevention, early identification and response", 2nd edition <http://www.nedc.com.au/files/Resources/Teachers%20Resource.pdf>

40. The National Eating Disorders Collaboration. (2012b), *Eating disorders in Australia.* Sydney: NEDC

41. Above, NEDC

42. Black Dog Institute and Mission Australia (2017), *Youth Mental Health Report – Youth Survey 2012–2016* <https://blackdoginstitute.org.au/docs/default-source/research/evidence-and-policy-section/2017-youth-mental-health-report_mission-australia-and-black-dog-institute.pdf?sfvrsn=6>

43. Trajillo, N (1995), Machines, missiles, and men: Images of the male body on ABC's "Monday Night Football", *Sociology of Sport Journal*, 12, pp. 403–423

44. McCabe, M and Ricciardelli, L (2001), Parent, peer and media influences on body image and strategies to both increase and decrease body size among adolescent boys and girls, *Adolescence*, pp. 36, 142, 225–240

45. Cusuman, D and Thompson, J (1997), Body image and body shape ideals in magazines: Exposure, awareness, and internalisation, *Sex Roles*, pp. 37, 701–721

46. Ibid.

47. Above, NEDC

48. Butterfly Foundation. (2012), *Paying the price: the economic and social impact of eating disorders in Australia.* Melbourne: Butterfly Foundation

49. Above, Cooke

50. Hay PJ, Mond J, Buttner P, Darby A (2008), *Eating Disorder Behaviors Are Increasing: Findings from Two Sequential Community Surveys in South Australia.* PLoS ONE 3(2): e1541. doi:10.1371/journal.pone.0001541

51. Cooke, K (2013), *Girl Stuff*, Penguin Random House Australia, p. 260

52. The Butterfly Foundation, "Body Image Tips for Boys" (PDF online) <https://thebutterflyfoundation.org.au/assets/Uploads/Factsheets/Body-Image-Tips-for-Boys.pdf>

53. The Butterfly Foundation, "Body Image Tips for Girls" (PDF online) <https://thebutterflyfoundation.org.au/assets/Uploads/Factsheets/Body-Image-Tips-for-Girls.pdf

54. The Butterfly Foundation, "Tips for Recovery" (PDF online) <https://thebutterflyfoundation.org.au/assets/Uploads/Factsheets/Tips-for-Recovery.pdf>

55. Reed, K et al (2016), "Helicopter parenting and emerging adult self-efficacy: implications for mental and physical health", *Journal of Child and Family Studies*, 25:10, pp. 3136–3149

56. Nelson, L et al (2015), "Is hovering smothering or loving? An examination of parental warmth as a moderator of relations between helicopter parenting and emerging adults' indices of adjustment", *Emerging Adulthood*, 3 (4)

57. NSW Department of Education, "Children thrive on parental involvement", *School at Oz* (online), date unknown <http://www.schoolatoz.nsw.edu.au/wellbeing/development/children-thrive-on-parental-involvement>

58. Dr Happy, "Is your child stressed at school?", *hif Healthy Lifestyle Blog* (online), 5 December 2016 <https://www.hif.com.au/healthy-lifestyle-blog/mental-health/05122016/is-your-child-stressed-at-school.aspx>

59. Jerome Doraisamy, "Sleeping your way to the top", *Lawyers Weekly* (online), 27 March 2017, <https://www.lawyersweekly.com.au/opinion/20813-sleeping-your-way-to-the-top>

60. Winsler et al, *Sleepless in Fairfax: The Difference One More Hour of Sleep Can Make for Teen Hopelessness, Suicidal Ideation, and Substance Use* (2015), *Journal of Youth and Adolescence*, 44: 362

61. Ibid.

62. Dr Sarah Blunden, "Adolescent Sleep Facts Sheet", Sleep Education Australia (online), date unknown <http://www.sleepeducation.net.au/Docs/Adolescent's%20Sleep%20Facts%20Sheet.pdf>

63. Ibid.

64. Pot et al, "The effects of partial sleep deprivation on energy balance: a systematic review and meta-analysis" (2017), *European Journal of Clinical Nutrition* 71, pp. 614–624

65. Laschon, E. "Mobile phone are tempting teens late at night – and researchers say it's causing problems", ABC News (online), 30 May 2017 <http://www.abc.net.au/news/2017-05-30/mobile-phone-use-late-at-night-causing-teens-problems-study-says/8572682>

66. Dr. Sarah Blunden, "Adolescent Sleep Facts Sheet", Sleep Education Australia (online), date unknown <http://www.sleepeducation.net.au/Docs/Adolescent's%20Sleep%20Facts%20Sheet.pdf>

67. Cooke, K (2007), *Girl Stuff*, Penguin Random House Australia, p. 245

68. Ito M., Horst, H., Bittani, M., Boyd, d., Herr-Stephenson, B., Lange, P.G., Tripp, L. (2008), *Living and Learning With New Media: Summary of Findings From the Digital Youth Project.* Chicago, IL: John D. and Catherine T. MacArthur Foundation Reports on Digital Media and Learning.

69. Gonzales et al, "Mirror, mirror on my Facebook wall: effects of exposure to Facebook on self-esteem", *Cyberpsychol Behav Soc Network* (2011), 14: pp. 79–83

70. Rideout, V.J., Foehr, U.G., & Roberts, D.F. (2010), Generation M2: Media in the lives of 8–18 year olds. Retrieved on May 15, 2011 from Kaiser Family Foundation website: <http://www.kff.org/entmedia/upload/8010.pdf>

71. Carroll, J et al (2011), *Impact of social media on adolescent behavioural health*, Oakland, CA: California Adolescent Health Collaborative

72. Boyar, R., Levine, D., & Zensius, N. (2011), Tech SexUSA: *Youth Sexuality and Reproductive Health in the Digital Age.* <http://www.isis-inc.org/ISISpaper_techsx_usa.pdf>

73. Lenhart, A., Ling, R., Campbell, S., & Purcell, K. (2010), *Teens & mobile phones. Pew Internet & American*

Life Project. <http://www.pewinternet.org/Reports/2010/Teens-and-Mobile-Phones.aspx>

74. Liz Claiborne, Inc. (2008), *Tween and Teen Dating Violence and Abuse Study.* <http://loveisnotabuse.com/c/document_library/get_file?p_l_id=45693&folderId=72612&nam e=DLFE-203.pdf>

75. Sex and Tech: Results of a Survey of Teens and Young Adults. Washington, DC: Retrieved from *National Campaign to Prevent Teen and Unplanned Pregnancy* website: http://www.thenationalcampaign.org/sextech/pdf/sextech_summary.pdf

76. Clifford, S. (2009, February 7), Straight talk on digital harassment for teenagers. *The New York Times* (online) <http://www.nytimes.com/2009/01/27/technology/27iht-adco.1.19705877.html>

77. Bates, S (2017), Revenge Porn and Mental Health: A Qualitative Analysis of the Mental Health Effects of Revenge Porn on Female Survivors, *Feminist Criminology*, 12 (1), 22–42

78. Kaltiala-Heino et al, *Bullying, depression and suicidal ideation in Finnish adolescents: school survey* (1999), BMJ pp. 319–348

79. Espelage et al, *Homophobic teasing, psychological outcomes, and sexual orientation among high school students: what influence do parents and schools have?* (2008), School Psychology Review, 37–2 pp. 202–216

80. Wilkinson, R et al (2003), *Social Determinants of Health – The Solid Facts*, World Health Organisation, Geneva

81. Boulton, M et al (1994), "Bully/victim problems in middle-school children: stability, self-perceived competence, peer perceptions and peer acceptance", *Br J Dev Psychol*, 12: 315–329

82. Perren et al, Bullying in school and cyberspace: associations with depressive symptoms in Swiss and Australian adolescents (2010), *Child and Adolescent Psychiatry and Mental Health*, 4 (28)

83. Blumenfeld, W.J. and Cooper, R.M. (2010), LGBT and Allied Youth Responses to Cyberbullying: Policy Implications. *The International Journal of Critical Pedagogy*, 3(1), 114–133. <http://freireproject.org/images/2321/IJCPv3_7.pdf>

84. Ibid.

85. Blumenfeld, W.J. and Cooper, R.M. (2010), LGBT and Allied Youth Responses to Cyberbullying: Policy Implications. *The International Journal of Critical Pedagogy*, 3(1), 114–133. <http://freireproject.org/images/2321/IJCPv3_7.pdf>

86. Kim YS, et al (2005), "School bullying and suicidal risk in Korean middle school students", *Pediatrics*, 115(2): 357–363

87. Black Dog Institute and Mission Australia (2017), *Youth Mental Health Report – Youth Survey 2012–2016* <https://blackdoginstitute.org.au/docs/default-source/research/evidence-and-policy-section/2017-youth-mental-health-report_mission-australia-and-black-dog-institute.pdf?sfvrsn=6>

88. MindHealthConnect, "Sexuality and mental health", healthdirect.gov.au (online), August 2015 <http://www.mindhealthconnect.org.au/sexuality-mental-health>

89. Heart Foundation, "Looking after yourself", *Heart Foundation* (online), date unknown <https://www.heartfoundation.org.au/your-heart/living-with-heart-disease/looking-after-yourself>

90. Brody, S (2006), "Blood pressure reactivity to stress is better for people who recently had penile-vaginal intercourse than for people who had other or no sexual activity", *Biological Psychology*, 71: 214–22

91. Charnetski, CJ et al (2004), "Sexual frequency and salivary immunoglobulin A (IgA)", *Psychology Report*, 94: 839–844

92. Lindau, ST et al (2007), "A study of sexuality and health among older adults in the United States", *New England Journal of Medicine*, 357: 762–774

93. Cohen et al (2015), "Does hugging provide stress-buffering social support? A study of susceptibility to upper respiratory infection and illness", *Psychol Sci*, 26 (2), 135–147

94. Meier, AM (2007), "Adolescent first sex and subsequent mental health", *American Journal of Sociology*, 112 (6), 1811–1847

95. Mendle, J et al (2013), "Depression and adolescent sexual activity in romantic and non-romantic relational contexts: a genetically-informative sibling comparison", *Journal of Abnormal Psychology*, 122 (1), 51–63

96. Sandberg-Thoma, SE et al (2014), "Casual sexual relationships and mental health in adolescence and emerging adulthood", *The Journal of Sex Research*, 51 (2), 121–130

97. Grodsky, E et al (year unknown), "Adolescent sex, mental health and academic engagement: the role of norms", citation unknown – sourced from <http://paa2012.princeton.edu/papers/122192>

98. Rudolph, KD (2002), "Gender differences in emotional responses to interpersonal stress during adolescence", *Journal of Adolescent Health*, 30S: 3–13

99. Above, Grodsky et al

100. Bennett, D et al (2000), "Adolescent mental health and risky sexual behaviour", *BMJ*, 321: 251–252

101. Better Health Channel, "Teenagers and sexual issues", Victoria State Government (online), date unknown <https://www.betterhealth.vic.gov.au/health/healthyliving/teenagers-and-sexual-issues>

102. Manson, M "7 things sex education should have taught us but didn't", 2 October 2013 (online) <https://markmanson.net/sex-education>

103. Butler 1980, Young Wech Bakema 1989

104. Workman, M and Beer, J (1989), "Self-esteem, depression, and alcohol dependency among high school students", *Psychological Reports*, 65, 451–455

105. Ibid.

106. Read, S (1974), *Winston Churchill Reporting: adventures of a young war correspondent*, Da Capo Press, Boston MA

107. Holsman, J (2016), *The high school survival guide – your roadmap to: studying, socialising, succeeding*, Mango Media Inc, p. 167

108. "An emerging adolescent health risk: Caffeinated energy drink consumption patterns among high school students", *Preventative Medicine*, Volume 62, pp. 54–59, May 2014

109. Energy drinks linked to teen depression and drug use <https://uwaterloo.ca/stories/energy-drinks-linked-teen-depression-and-drug-use>

110. Lieberman, M et al (2007), "Putting Feelings into Words" – Research Article, *Association for Psychological Science*, Volume 18 Number 5, pp. 421–428

111. Sample, I "Keeping a diary makes you happier", *The Guardian* (online), 15 February 2009 <https://www.theguardian.com/science/2009/feb/15/psychology-usa>

112. Above, re Lieberman

113. Ibid.

114. Krentzman, A et al (2015), "Feasibility, acceptability, and impact of a web-based gratitude exercise among individuals in outpatient treatment for alcohol use disorder", *The Journal of Positive Psychology*, Vol. 10, Issue 6

115. ReachOut, "How to set goals", ReachOut.com (online), date unknown, <http://au.reachout.com/how-to-set-goals>

116. Ariga, A., & Lleras, A. Brief and rare mental "breaks" keep you focused: Deactivation and reactivation of task goals preempt vigilance decrements. *Cognition* (2011), doi:10.1016/j.cognition.2010.12.007

117. Kang, S (2016), "Spaced Repetition Promotes Efficient and Effective Learning: Policy Implications for Instruction", *Policy Insights from the Behavioural and Brain Sciences*, 3(1), 12–19

118. Knight, S (2016), *Get Your Sh*t Together*, Hachette UK, London, p. 113

119. Lenhart A, Purcell K, Smith A., & Zickuhr K. (2010), Social media & mobile internet use among teens and young adults. *Pew Internet & American Life Project*. <http://www.pewinternet.org/Reports/2010/Social-Media-and-Young-Adults.aspx>

120. Desha, L et al (2007), "Physical activity and depressive symptoms in American adolescents", *Journal of Sport & Exercise Physiology*, 29 (4) 534–543

121. Ibid.

122. Guszkowska, M (2004), "Effects of exercise on anxiety, depression and mood", *Psychiatr Pol*, 38: 611–620

123. Callaghan, P (2004), "Exercise: a neglected intervention in mental health care?" *J Psychiatr Ment Health Nurs*, 11: 476–483

124. Hallal, P et al (2006), "Adolescent physical activity and health: a systematic review", *Sports Medicine*, 36 (12), 1019–1030

125. Mahoney, J et al (2002), "Structured after-school activities as a moderator od depressed mood for adolescents with detached relations to their parents", *Journal of Community Psychology*, 30 (1), 69–86

126. Eime, R et al (2013), "A systematic review of the psychological and social benefits of participation in sport for children and adolescents: informing development of a conceptual model of health through sport", *International Journal of Behavioural Nutrition and Physical Activity*, 10:98

127. Bratman, G et al (2015), "Nature experience reduces rumination and subgenual prefrontal cortex activation", *Proceedings of the National Academy of Science*, 112: 28, 8567–8572

128. Kirkwood, G et al (2005), "Yoga for anxiety: a systematic review of the research", *British Journal of Sports Medicine*, 39 (12), 884–891

129. Harvard Medical School, "Yoga for anxiety and depression", *Harvard Medical Publications* (online), April 2009 <http://www.health.harvard.edu/mind-and-mood/yoga-for-anxiety-and-depression>

130. Pilkington, K et al (2005), "Yoga for depression: the research evidence", *Journal of Affective Disorders*, 89 (1–3), 13–24

131. Khalsa, SB et al (2012), "Evaluation of the mental health benefits of yoga in a secondary school: a preliminary randomized controlled trial", *J Behav Health Serv Res*, 39 (1), 80–90

132. Gururaja, D et al (2011), "Effect of yoga on mental health: comparative study between young and senior subjects in Japan", *International Journal of Yoga*, 4 (1), 7–12

133. O'Connor, PJ et al (2010), "Mental health benefits of strength training in adults", *American Journal of Lifestyle Medicine*, 4 (5), 377–396

134. Knight, S (2016), *Get Your Sh*t Together*, Hachette UK, London, p. 189

135. Dr Roopleen, *Motivational Quotes* (online), date unknown <http://www.drroopleen.com/motivational-quotes/>

136. Waters, L et al (2015), Contemplative Education: a systematic, evidence-based review of the effect of meditation interventions in schools, *Educational Psychology Review*, 27, 103–134

137. Huppert, F et al (2010), A controlled trial of mindfulness training in schools; the importance of practice for an impact on wellbeing. *The Journal of Positive Psychology*, 5 (4), 264–274

138. Silber, E "What's the deal with adult colouring books?", *Psychology Today*, 25 November 2016 (online) <https://www.psychologytoday.com/articles/201609/what-s-the-deal-adult-coloring-books>

139. Ibid.

140. Dunn, C and Hall, T (2017), "Episode 1: Escape the Cult of Busy!", *Crappy to Happy* (podcast), 14 August 2017 <https://itunes.apple.com/au/podcast/crappy-to-happy/id1274672540?mt=2>

141. Broderick, P et al (2009), Learning to BREATHE: A pilot trial of a mindfulness curriculum for adolescents, *Advances in School Mental Health Promotion*, 2 (1), 35–45

142. Lau, N et al (2011), Preliminary outcomes of a mindfulness-based programme for Hong Kong adolescents in schools: well-being, stress and depressive symptoms, *International Journal of Children's Spirituality*, 16 (4), 315–330

143. Mendelson, T et al (2010), Feasibility and preliminary outcomes of a school-based mindfulness intervention for urban youth, *Journal of Abnormal Child Psychology*, 38 (7), 985–994

144. Bogels, S et al (2008), Mindfulness training for adolescents with externalising disorders and their parents, *Behavioural and Cognitive Psychotherapy*, 36 (2), 193–209

145. Dunn, C and Hall, T (2017), "Episode 1: Escape the Cult of Busy!", *Crappy to Happy* (podcast), 14 August 2017 <https://itunes.apple.com/au/podcast/crappy-to-happy/id1274672540?mt=2>

146. Waters, L (2011), "A review of school-based positive psychology interventions", *The Australian Educational and Developmental Psychologist*, 28 (2), 75–90

147. Seligman, M et al (2000), "Positive psychology: an introduction", *American Psychologist*, 55, 5–14

148. Gable, S et al (2005), "What (and why) is positive psychology?", *General Psychology*, 9, 103–110

149. Waters, L (2011), "A review of school-based positive psychology interventions", *The Australian Educational and Developmental Psychologist*, 28 (2), 75–90

150. Durlack, JA et al (2011), "The impact of enhancing students' social and emotional learning: a meta-analysis of school-based universal interventions", *Child Development*, 82 (1), 405–432

151. Waters, L (2011), "A review of school-based positive psychology interventions", *The Australian Educational and Developmental Psychologist*, 28 (2), 75–90

152. Manson, M "Stop trying to be happy", 10 October 2013 (online) <https://markmanson.net/stop-trying-to-be-happy>

153. Dr Happy, "3 ways to harness positive psychology for a more resilient you", 3 April 2013 (online) <http://www.drhappy.com.au/2013/04/03/3-positive-psychology-strategies-for-building-more-resilience/>

154. Thomas Oppong, "The incredible power of a productive pause", *The Medium*, 17 August 2017 (online) <https://medium.com/the-mission/take-a-productive-pause-40eace753ff5>

155. Dr Roopleen, "Motivational Quotes", date unknown (online) <http://www.drroopleen.com/motivational-quotes/>

156. Lea Waters, "Getting the happiness formula right in the classroom", *The Conversation* (online), 6 May 2011 <https://theconversation.com/getting-the-happiness-formula-right-in-the-classroom-370>

157. FACT SHEET, "Music and mental health", ReachOut (online), date unknown <http://au.reachout.com/music-and-mental-health>

158. Virtue, R "Using music to help Aboriginal youth manage mental illness", ABC Newcastle (online), 24 May 2016 <http://www.abc.net.au/news/2016-05-24/using-music-to-help-aboriginal-youth-manage-mental-illness/7437014>

159. Bartlett, L-M "Mental health in Music", SANE Australia (online), 21 March 2016 <https://www.sane.org/media-centre/the-sane-blog/1723-mental-health-in-music>

160. Ibid.

161. Addison, J and Steele, Sir R (1709), *The Tatler*, London

162. Ibid.

163. Lewis, D (2009), "Galaxy Stress Research", Mindlab International, Sussex University, UK

164. Ibid.

165. Ibid.

166. Kidd, D and Castano, E (2013), "Reading literary fiction improves theory of mind", *Science*, 342: 6156, 377–380

167. Wilson, R et al (2013), "Life-span cognitive activity, neuropathologic burden, and cognitive ageing", *Neurology*, 81: 4, 314–321

168. Mar, R et al (2009), "Exploring the link between reading fiction and empathy: ruling out individual differences and examining outomes", *Communications*, 34, 407–428

169. Knight, S (2016), *Get Your Sh*t Together*, Hachette UK, London, pp. 209–210

170. Cooke, K (2013), *Girl Talk*, Penguin Random House Australia, p. 249

171. Ibid., p. 252

172. Rickwood, D et al (2005), "Young people's help-seeking for mental health problems", *Australian e-journal for the Advancement of Mental Health*, 4 (3), 1–34

173. Gulliver, A et al (2010), "Perceived barriers and facilitators to mental health help-seeking in young people: a systematic review", *BMC Psychiatry*, 10: 113

174. Ibid.

175. Vogl G., Ratnaike D., Ivancic L., Rowley A. & Chandy V. (2016), *One Click Away? Insights into Mental Health Digital Self-help by Young Australians*. Sydney: EY and ReachOut Australia

176. Ibid.

Select bibliography

Books

Addison, Joseph and Steele, Richard, Sir (1709), *The Tatler*, London
Cooke, K (2013), *Girl Stuff*, Penguin Random House Australia
Dunn, M (2016), *Letters to Mitch*, self-published, pp. 192–194
Holsman, J (2016), *The High School Survival Guide*, Mango Media, Inc
Knight, S (2016), *Get Your Sh*t Together*, Hachette UK, London
Lewis, D (2009), "*Galaxy Stress Research*", Mindlab International, Sussex University, UK
Read, S (1974), *Winston Churchill Reporting: adventures of a young war correspondent*, Da Capo Press, Boston MA

Reports

Australian Institute of Health and Welfare (2011), *Young Australians: their health and wellbeing*, 2011, Cat. no. (PHE 140), Canberra: AIHW
Black Dog Institute and Mission Australia (2017), *Youth Mental Health Report – Youth Survey 2012–2016*
Butterfly Foundation (2012), *Paying the price: the economic and social impact of eating disorders in Australia.* Melbourne: Butterfly Foundation
Carroll, J et al (2011), Impact of social media on adolescent behavioural health, Oakland, CA: *California Adolescent Health Collaborative*
Cowan, G (2013), *The elephant in the boardroom: getting mentally fit for work*
Lawrence D et al (2015), *The Mental Health of Children and Adolescents – Report on the second Australian Child and Adolescent Survey of Mental Health and Wellbeing.* Canberra: Department of Health
Leonard et al, *Private Lives 2: the second national survey of the health and wellbeing of gay, lesbian, bisexual and transgender (GLBT) Australians* (2012), Australian Research Centre in Sex, Health and Society, La Trobe University, Melbourne
National Eating Disorders Collaboration, "Eating disorders in schools: prevention, early identification and response", 2nd edition
Slade T, Johnston A, Teesson M, Whiteford H, Burgess P, Pirkis J, et al (2009), *The Mental Health of Australians 2: Report on the 2007 National Survey of Mental Health and Wellbeing.* Canberra: Department of Health and Ageing
Vogl G., Ratnaike D., Ivancic L., Rowley A. & Chandy V. (2016), *One Click Away? Insights into Mental Health Digital Self-help by Young Australians.* Sydney: EY and ReachOut Australia

Studies

Arboleda-Florez, J (2002), "What causes stigma?", *World Psychiatry*, 1(1) 25–26
Ariga, A., & Lleras, A. Brief and rare mental "breaks" keep you focused: Deactivation and reactivation of task goals preempt vigilance decrements. *Cognition* (2011), doi:10.1016/j.cognition.2010.12.007
Australian Bureau of Statistics (2016), *Causes of death, 2015* Cat. no. 3303.0. ABS: Canberra
Australian Bureau of Statistics (2007), National Survey of Mental Health and Wellbeing: Summary of results. 4236.0, Australian Government, Canberra
Australian Institute of Health and Welfare (2011), *Young Australians: their health and wellbeing*, 2011. Cat. no. (PHE 140), Canberra: AIHW
Bates, S (2017), Revenge Porn and Mental Health: A Qualitative Analysis of the Mental Health Effects of Revenge Porn on Female Survivors, *Feminist Criminology*, 12 (1), 22–42
Bennett, D et al (2000), "Adolescent mental health and risky sexual behaviour", *BMJ*, 321: 251–252
Blumenfeld, W.J. and Cooper, R.M. (2010), LGBT and Allied Youth Responses to Cyberbullying: Policy Implications. The International Journal of Critical Pedagogy, 3(1), 114–133
Bogels, S et al (2008), Mindfulness training for adolescents with externalising disorders and their parents, *Behavioural and Cognitive Psychotherapy*, 36 (2), 193–209

Boulton, M et al (1994), "Bully/victim problems in middle-school children: stability, self-perceived competence, peer perceptions and peer acceptance", *Br J Dev Psychol*, 12: 315–329

Bratman, G et al (2015), "Nature experience reduces rumination and subgenual prefrontal cortex activation", *Proceedings of the National Academy of Science*, 112: 28, 8567–8572

Broderick, P et al (2009), Learning to BREATHE: A pilot trial of a mindfulness curriculum for adolescents, *Advances in School Mental Health Promotion*, 2 (1), 35–45

Brody, S (2006), "Blood pressure reactivity to stress is better for people who recently had penile-vaginal intercourse than for people who had other or no sexual activity", *Biological Psychology*, 71: 214–22

Callaghan, P (2004), "Exercise: a neglected intervention in mental health care?" *J Psychiatr Ment Health Nurs*, 11: 476–483

Charnetski, CJ et al (2004), "Sexual frequency and salivary immunoglobulin A (IgA)", *Psychology Report*, 94: 839–844

Cohen et al (2015), "Does hugging provide stress-buffering social support? A study of susceptibility to upper respiratory infection and illness", *Psychol Sci*, 26 (2), 135–147

Cusuman, D and Thompson, J (1997), Body image and body shape ideals in magazines: Exposure, awareness, and internalisation, *Sex Roles*, 37, 701–721

Desha, L et al (2007), "Physical activity and depressive symptoms in American adolescents", *Journal of Sport & Exercise Physiology*, 29 (4) 534–543

Durlack, JA et al (2011), "The impact of enhancing students' social and emotional learning: a meta-analysis of school-based universal interventions", *Child Development*, 82 (1), 405–432

Dyson et al, *Don't ask, don't tell. Report of the same-sex attracted youth suicide data collection project* (2003), Australian Research Centre in Sex, Health and Society, La Trobe University, Melbourne

Eime, R et al (2013), "A systematic review of the psychological and social benefits of participation in sport for children and adolescents: informing development of a conceptual model of health through sport", *International Journal of Behavioural Nutrition and Physical Activity*, 10:98

Espelage et al, *Homophobic teasing, psychological outcomes, and sexual orientation among high school students: what influence do parents and schools have?* (2008), School Psychology Review, 37–2 pp. 202–216

Gable, S et al (2005), "What (and why) is positive psychology?", *General Psychology*, 9, 103–110

Gonzales et al, "Mirror, mirror on my Facebook wall: effects of exposure to Facebook on self-esteem", *Cyberpsychol Behav Soc Network* (2011), 14: 79–83

Gulliver, A et al (2010), "Perceived barriers and facilitators to mental health help-seeking in young people: a systematic review", *BMC Psychiatry*, 10: 113

Gururaja, D et al (2011), "Effect of yoga on mental health: comparative study between young and senior subjects in Japan", *International Journal of Yoga*, 4 (1), 7–12

Guszkowska, M (2004), "Effects of exercise on anxiety, depression and mood", *"Psychiatr Pol*, 38: 611–620

Hallal, P et al (2006), "Adolescent physical activity and health: a systematic review", *Sports Medicine*, 36 (12), 1019–1030

Hay PJ, Mond J, Buttner P, Darby A (2008), Eating Disorder Behaviors Are Increasing: Findings from Two Sequential Community Surveys in South Australia. PLoS ONE 3(2): e1541. doi:10.1371/journal.pone.0001541

Huppert, F et al (2010), A controlled trial of mindfulness training in schools; the importance of practice for an impact on wellbeing. *The Journal of Positive Psychology*, 5 (4), 264–274

Ito M., Horst, H., Bittani, M., Boyd, D., Herr-Stephenson, B., Lange, P.G., Tripp, L. (2008), Living and Learning With New Media: Summary of Findings From the Digital Youth Project. Chicago, IL: *John D. and Catherine T. MacArthur Foundation Reports on Digital Media and Learning*

Kaltiala-Heino et al, *Bullying, depression and suicidal ideation in Finnish adolescents: school survey* (1999), BMJ pp. 319–348

Kang, S (2016), "Spaced Repetition Promotes Efficient and Effective Learning: Policy Implications for Instruction", *Policy Insights from the Behavioural and Brain Sciences*, 3(1), 12–19

Kessler, RD et al (2005), *Lifetime prevalence and age-of-onset distributions of DSM-IV disorders in the National Comorbidity Survey Replication.* Archives of General Psychiatry, 62: p. 593–602

Khalsa, SB et al (2012), "Evaluation of the mental health benefits of yoga in a secondary school: a preliminary randomized controlled trial", *J Behav Health Serv Res*, 39 (1), 80–90

Kidd, D and Castano, E (2013), "Reading literary fiction improves theory of mind", *Science*, 342: 6156, 377–380

Kim YS, et al (2005), "School bullying and suicidal risk in Korean middle school students", *Pediatrics*, 115(2): 357–363

Kirkwood, G et al (2005), "Yoga for anxiety: a systematic review of the research", *British Journal of Sports Medicine*, 39 (12), 884–891

Krentzman, A et al (2015), "Feasibility, acceptability, and impact of a web-based gratitude exercise among individuals in outpatient treatment for alcohol use disorder", *The Journal of Positive Psychology*, Vol. 10, Issue 6

Lau, N et al (2011), Preliminary outcomes of a mindfulness-based programme for Hong Kong adolescents in schools: well-being, stress and depressive symptoms, *International Journal of Children's Spirituality*, 16 (4), 315–330.

Lieberman, M et al (2007), "Putting Feelings into Words" – Research Article, *Association for Psychological Science*, Volume 18 Number 5, pp. 421–428

Lindau, ST et al (2007), "A study of sexuality and health among older adults in the United States", *New England Journal of Medicine*, 357: 762–774

Mahoney, J et al (2002), "Structured after-school activities as a moderator of depressed mood for adolescents with detached relations to their parents", *Journal of Community Psychology*, 30 (1), 69–86

Mar, R et al (2009), "Exploring the link between reading fiction and empathy: ruling out individual differences and examining outcomes", *Communications*, 34, 407–428

McCabe, M and Ricciardelli, L (2001), Parent, peer and media influences on body image and strategies to both increase and decrease body size among adolescent boys and girls, *Adolescence*, 36, 142, 225–240

MediaCom Melbourne (2015), *Youthbeyondblue Anxiety and Depression Ad Tracking Survey Post Campaign Research*

Meier, AM (2007), "Adolescent first sex and subsequent mental health", *American Journal of Sociology*, 112 (6), 1811–1847

Mendle, J et al (2013), "Depression and adolescent sexual activity in romantic and non-romantic relational contexts: a genetically-informative sibling comparison", *Journal of Abnormal Psychology*, 122 (1), 51–63

Mendelson, T et al (2010), Feasibility and preliminary outcomes of a school-based mindfulness intervention for urban youth, *Journal of Abnormal Child Psychology*, 38 (7), 985–994

Nelson, L et al (2015), "Is hovering smothering or loving? An examination of parental warmth as a moderator of relations between helicopter parenting and emerging adults' indices of adjustment", *Emerging Adulthood* 3 (4)

O'Connor, PJ et al (2010), "Mental health benefits of strength training in adults", *American Journal of Lifestyle Medicine*, 4 (5), 377–396

Perren et al, *Bullying in school and cyberspace: associations with depressive symptoms in Swiss and Australian adolescents* (2010), Child and Adolescent Psychiatry and Mental Health, 4 (28)

Pilkington, K et al (2005), "Yoga for depression: the research evidence", *Journal of Affective Disorders*, 89 (1–3), 13–24

Pot et al, "The effects of partial sleep deprivation on energy balance: a systematic review and meta-analysis" (2017), *European Journal of Clinical Nutrition* 71, 614–624

Reed, K et al (2016), "Helicopter parenting and emerging adult self-efficacy: implications for mental and physical health", *Journal of Child and Family Studies*, 25:10, 3136–3149

Rickwood, D et al (2005), "Young people's help-seeking for mental health problems", *Australian e-journal for the Advancement of Mental Health*, 4 (3), 1–34

Rudolph, KD (2002), "Gender differences in emotional responses to interpersonal stress during adolescence", *Journal of Adolescent Health*, 30S: 3–13

Sandberg-Thoma, SE et al (2014), "Casual sexual relationships and mental health in adolescence and emerging adulthood", *The Journal of Sex Research*, 51 (2), 121–130

Seligman, M et al (2000), "Positive psychology: an introduction", *American Psychologist*, 55, 5–14

Trajillo, N (1995), Machines, missiles, and men: Images of the male body on ABC's "Monday Night Football", *Sociology of Sport Journal*, 12, 403–423

Waters, L (2011), "A review of school-based positive psychology interventions", *The Australian Educational and Developmental Psychologist*, 28 (2), 75–90

Waters, L et al (2015), Contemplative Education: a systematic, evidence-based review of the effect of meditation interventions in schools, *Educational Psychology Review*, 27, 103–134

Wilson, R et al (2013), "Life-span cognitive activity, neuropathologic burden, and cognitive ageing", *Neurology*, 81: 4, 314–321

Winsler et al, *Sleepless in Fairfax: The Difference One More Hour of Sleep Can Make for Teen Hopelessness, Suicidal Ideation*, and Substance Use (2015), Journal of Youth and Adolescence, 44: 362

Workman, M and Beer, J (1989), "Self-esteem, depression, and alcohol dependency among high school students", *Psychological Reports*, 65, 451–455

Podcasts

Dunn, C and Hall, T (2017), "Episode 1: Escape the Cult of Busy!", *Crappy to Happy* (podcast), 14 August 2017 <https://itunes.apple.com/au/podcast/crappy-to-happy/id1274672540?mt=2>

Acknowledgements

I never planned to write a second *Wellness Doctrines* title. My first book, aimed at lawyers and law students, was a cathartic passion project which I saw as being the final step in my recovery, after which I'd go back to a real job. I couldn't have anticipated the path I'd go down following publication of that title in October 2015.

But even with newfound publishing and advocacy experience under my belt, the writing of this second book wasn't easy. In fact, it was a lot harder. Without assistance and support from a great many people in my life, both personally and professionally, the second *Wellness Doctrines* title wouldn't be in your hands right now.

A big thank you to my publishers, Brio Books. Rod and Jon, I really appreciate you getting on board with this second title, and I'm even more grateful for the kind, compassionate and hospitable way you do business. Your approach has made this whole process so much easier for me, and I hope I haven't been too difficult to work with!

To everyone who contributed – those who wrote beautiful

testimonials, those who generously gave up their time to be interviewed, and those whose research I relied upon to shape my arguments – it means so much to me that you'd be willing to contribute to this project, and I can't thank you enough.

I am most appreciative to Dr Tim Sharp who penned the Expert's note. Your contribution brought credibility and authority to this book that I couldn't bring myself, and I am so thankful to you for lending your name, and your voice, to my work. It means so much to me.

To my parents, Ted and Nas – thanks for your unwavering love and support, especially at times when I don't ask for it and don't want to listen. I'm very grateful for everything you do for me. To Oliver, Isabel and Emma, my siblings and sister-in-law – thanks for always checking in and seeing how I'm doing, and for backing me in chasing these professional dreams. I truly value it! And to the rest of my family, as well as a number of family friends, thank you for your consistent words of encouragement and advice.

To my friends, especially my Aloys mates – thank you for always having my back and being there in times of strife, and for all the love, laughter and fun. I'm fortunate to have a wide circle of mates, but I especially need to thank the following people: Angus and Lucy, Michael and Nushi, Codie and Chloe, Jack and Gill, Luke and Dom, Aleks, Sean, Pat, Dan and Jacqui, Dan and Lisa, Will and Dani, Alex, Katie, Christy, Camellia, Leesa, and Dave. I'm worried that I've missed out someone important (I'm so sorry if I have), but to all my friends who have been there for me, thank you from the bottom of my heart.

To my professional mentors – Clarissa, Amanda, Maciek, Terry, Rachael, David, Nick, Paul, Maxine, Kate, Sam, Anna – thank you for everything that you do for me. It may seem like sometimes my personal and professional concerns go in circles, but I assure you, every conversation I have with you about my journey is invaluable in shaping who I am and where I'm headed. I'm truly grateful for your presence in my life.

I also need to mention Katie Bennett and Graeme Cowan, without whom my first book would never have come to fruition, and therefore this second one wouldn't exist either. Thank you for providing the inspiration for these writing projects. And to Laurine Croasdale, thank you for your wisdom and guidance along the way with my writing; your expertise has been a godsend.

Thanks to the legends at batyr for their partnership on this book project, and for the collaborative support that is still to come. Special shout-outs to Sam, Tim, Seb, Dave, Jenya and Nic for being so cool about everything. I'm thrilled to be able to work with you on this book, and I look forward to everything that is yet to come!

To all my colleagues in the mental health sphere – thank you for all the work you do in shining a light on these very serious ailments, for continually inspiring me, and for your collegiality and friendship. Amba, Marshall, Zoie, Anna, Mitch, Michelle, Marie, Cindy and many others … please keep up your important work. It motivates me to be better, and – more importantly – it helps countless Australians be healthier and happier.

Thank you to my alma mater, St Aloysius' College. Even though I have written that, in all likelihood, my mental health issues started percolating during high school (before boiling over while at university), I have nothing but fond memories of my time at Aloys. The holistic, well-rounded education I received, together with the extraordinary sense of community both at the College and in life after, has helped shape the man

I am today; in particular, a desire to be a man for others. My best mates are – and will always be – those from Aloys, and for that I am immensely thankful.

And finally, a big thanks to you, the reader. I'm so glad that you picked up this book, whether you got it through your school, your parents, or discovered it yourself. I truly hope you find it useful, and that it makes your schooling experience easier than it was for many who have come before you.